Tribute to the Confederate Secret Service

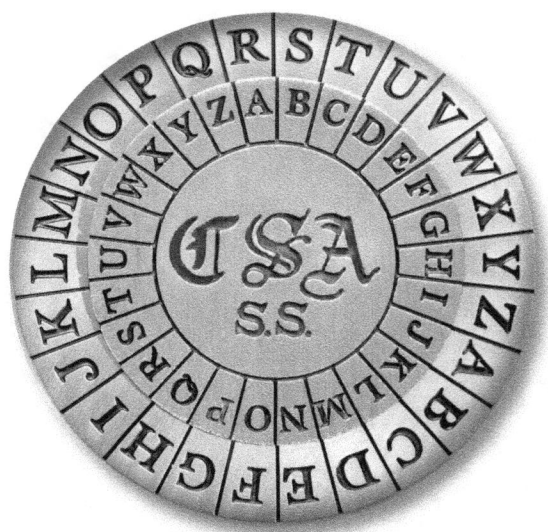

By Ted Boyias, Ph.D

Wake Forest, NC
www.scuppernongpress.com

I would like to thank Dr Vern Padgett for helping me. Janet Fiore whose two references books vol 1-2, *Self professed Confederate Obituaries* and *U. S. Newspaper Mentions,* were a valuable guide through 7,000 obituaries. I would like to thank Jay Gillette and John D. Klinedist who were there for me through this very tiring project. And last but not least, my publisher, Frank B. Powell, III, without whose assistance this book would not have been possible.

Tribute to the Confederate Secret Service
Ted Boyias, Ph.D

Copyright © 2025 Ted Boyias, Ph.D

First Printing

The Scuppernong Press
PO Box 1724
Wake Forest, NC 27588
www.scuppernongpress.com

Cover and book design by Frank B. Powell, III

All rights reserved

Printed in the United States of America

No part of this book may be reproduced or transmitted in any form or by any means, electronic or mechanical, including photocopying, recording, or by any information and storage and retrieval system, without written permission from the editor and/or publisher.

International Standard Book Number ISBN 978-1-942806-75-2

Library of Congress Control Number: 2025945401

Table of Contents

Chapter One — Intelligence Departments Heads 1

Chapter Two — Confederate Spies 11

Chapter Three — Scouts 35

Chapter Four — Couriers 41

Chapter Five — Staff 45

Chapter Six — Partisan Rangers 53

Conclusion 71

Bibliography 73

Chapter One

Intelligence Departments
Heads of Those Departments

President Jefferson Davis — Confederate States of America

President Davis was nominally the head of the Confederate Secret Service, in other words he was called the head, but in fact he really controlled only his own intelligence network, where his agents reported back directly to him. The other networks functioned independently and were led by their own heads.

Departments and Intelligence Networks Headed by their own heads.

War Department Signal Bureau and Signal Corps Headed by Major William Norris (1820-1896). According to Col. Harold Mills, a former CIA intelligence officer: "This agency was headed by Major William Norris, a former Baltimore attorney, and had about 1,200 personnel. It provided the "secret line" for regular mail and escort service between Richmond and Washington. It also had a pool of agents to support field operations, an example being "Harrison" who was assigned to General Longstreet at Gettysburg like a modern-day Cryptologic Security Service or SIGINT support to combat operations. The Signal Bureau/Corps forwarded Messages from Confederate officials in Richmond to contacts in Canada and Europe." [1]

Other duties included gathering and reading Northern newspapers for valuable information found in them. They also ran a mail service sending documents using preachers as couriers and agents. And finally, they tapped, and intercepted Union telegraph lines.

Provost Marshall of Richmond / Department of Richmond

Brigadier General John H. Winder, (1800-1865).

Colonel Mills describes the duties the Provost Marshall had. "The Provost Marshall of Richmond was Brigadier General John H. Winder, CSA, who had been a West Point instructor of President Jefferson Davis. The organization had about one hundred people including the guards at Richmond hospitals. General Winder was responsible to (1) organize defenses of Richmond; (2) enforce the discipline of Confederate military personnel in Richmond, a classic provost Marshall function,; (3) detect Union spies, a counter-intelligence function; and (4) care for Union POWs." [2]

War Department Torpedo Bureau

General Gabriel Rains, CSA

"This bureau was authorized on October 31, 1862, and was headed by General Gabriel Rains, CSA. It was charged with the production and use of explosive devices, land mines, naval mines and "coal torpedoes." The Torpedo Bureau produced simple, easily concealed explosives that were hidden behind enemy lines. Coal torpedoes were hallow metal castings resembling lumps of coal that were filled with gun powder and placed in coal bunkers of enemy vessels. A typical coal torpedo was about 3/8;" thick, weighed about three to four pounds, and held three to four ounces of gun powder. The idea was to damage a ship's steam engine, or to cause a boiler explosion and fire. These were invented by Captain Thomas Edgeworth Courtenay, CSA. Reportedly, President Lincoln found one on President Jefferson's desk after the evacuation of Richmond. …" [3]

Tribute to the Confederate Secret Service

Navy Submarine Battery Service

Commander Matthew Fontaine Maury, CSN (1806-1873).
Lt. Hunter Davidson, CSN (1827- 1913).

Colonel Mills gives an accurate description of this department: "The Navy Submarine Battery Service was headed by Commander Mathew Fontaine Maury, CSN, and Lt. Hunter Davidson, CSN, and was responsible for the defense of the major Southern ports of Richmond, Wilmington, Charleston, Savannah, and Mobile. The service laid mine fields to defend the harbors against the Union fleet. The service also built torpedo boats to attack the naval blockade of the Confederacy and damaged or sank some forty US Navy vessels." [4]

War Department Strategy Bureau

Major William Norris (He also heads this department too.)

Colonel Mills tells us: "This bureau recruited men with ideas for new weapons. Or who had interest in operating behind enemy lines. Its covert agents were assisted by the Torpedo Bureau. Its personnel trained as secret agents in teams known as "destructionists" or a "strategic corps." These teams were sent to destroy targets of interest to a department commander." [5]

The Greenhow Group
(A very unique all female spy network of beautiful ladies).

Rose O'Neil Greenhow

In Colonel Mills opinion: "The Greenhow Group was organized by Governor John Letcher of Virginia, John B. Magruder and Thomas Jordan. Rose O'Neil. Greenhow was the widow of a US State Department official and wife of a prominent doctor. She was considered a heroine of the Confederacy." [6]

Cavalry Scouts of Major General J. E. B. Stuart, CSA

Major General Stuart

"Major General Stuart was the senior Cavalry commander for the Army of Northern Virginia, and as such, he worked closely with his commander General Robert E. Lee, CSA. Stuart undertook aggressive scouting missions to know where the enemy was and to help General Lee avoid surprise. Lee needed the scout information to hold the initiative over the Union forces. Stuart's scouts were often assigned Secret Service tasks." 7

Clandestine Operations in Canada, 1863 - 1866

Jacob Thompson (1810 -1885)
Brigadier General Edwin Gray Lee, CSA

"The clandestine operation in Canada was led by Jacob Thompson and Brigadier General Edwin Lee, CSA. They were responsible for collection of Union political intelligence at the national level, for political action and propaganda operations, to support the Northern/Union peace movement, and for sabotage and sedition." 8

(I am very familiar with this "Northwest conspiracy operation," I covered this Confederate Secret Service operation in my book, *The Knights of the Golden Circle in California*. One of the reasons why this conspiracy failed, was people in Richmond assigned the leadership to a man like Jacob Thompson, a tired old man in bad health, who was also very gullible and who fell prey to a host of con men who took his money and were never seen again.

Brigadier Lee, on the other was a very competent relative to Robert E. Lee, but even he could not save this secret mission. The military leadership of this operation was given to a young 23-year-old Thomas

Hines, a very capable, perhaps the most dangerous of all Confederate Secret Service agents. Personally handpicked by Secretary of War Judah P. Benjamin, who tried to incite a rebellion in the Northwest conspiracy (what we call the Midwest today), and who failed only because the army of thousands of Knights of the Golden Circle failed to materialize in these Midwest states.)

Clandestine Operations in Great Britain

James Bullock (1823-1901)

Colonel Mills describes these operations: "James Dunwoody Bullock was charged with buying and arming ships in Europe for the Confederate Navy. He was a businessman and former naval officer who had wide experience in naval affairs, merchant shipping, and naval armament. He procured / funded the commerce raiders that harassed Union / Yankee ships. Bullock also tried to buy two ironclad ships that were confiscated by Britain." [9]

Mosby's Partisans and Agents

Colonel John Singleton Mosby, CSA (1833-1916)

"Colonel John Singleton Mosby, CSA, led partisans and agents behind enemy lines for a variety of operational missions." Colonel Mills said:"The Confederates operated at least three intelligence networks in Washington — two by Colonel Mosby and one by the Secret Service Bureau. Initially, Confederate intelligence collection centered on Washington. As the war wore on, emphasis shifted to more tactical or clandestine operations." Colonel John Singleton Mosby ... the *Gray Ghost* was authorized to form the 43rd Battalion, Virginia Cavalry as Mosby's rangers, raiders, or scouts. His battalion of partisan Cavalry carried out lightning strikes on Union targets and then would blend into the civilian population. In a typical operation, twenty to eighty men went on small raids behind enemy lines in Northern Virginia from the Shenandoah Valley in the West to Alexandria in the East, mostly in Fauquier and Loudoun counties. Mosby's forces scouted for intelligence and disrupted enemy intelligence collection. This came to be known as Mosby's Confederacy." [10]

Secretary of State Judah Benjamin (1811-1884)

Colonel Mills gives us an informative picture of this very talented Confederate leader: "Secretary Judah Benjamin was known as the "brains" of the Confederacy. He served as Attorney General, Secretary of War, and mostly as Secretary of State. He directed and financed many secret operations and was a powerful advisor to President Davis. Being a very discreet attorney, Benjamin left no records and memoirs and did not write a book. He burned all his personal papers.

Judah Benjamin was born in the West Indies and was raised in Charleston, South Carolina. He was a child prodigy attending Yale Law school at age fourteen. His achievements included being a founder of the Illinois Central Railroad, a state legislator and planter, and a US senator representing Louisiana in 1852. He was suspected in the Lincoln assassination and fled to England where he lived out his life as a barrister. His daughter buried him in Paris." [11]

Governor John Letcher (1813-1884)

According to Colonel Mills this Governor played an important role in the Confederate Secret Service: "Governor Letcher of Virginia … was the earliest known Confederate agent recruiter. He laid the foundation for espionage in. Washington, DC, by setting up a network in DC including Rose Greenhow and taught her a twenty-six-symbol cipher for secure communication.

It is interesting to note Governor Letcher had time and access to DC in early 1861 due to the timing of the seceding Southern states." [12]

President Jefferson Davis (1807-1889)

Mills explains the role the President played in matters of intelligence: "President Jefferson Davis …was a key official in Confederate espionage against the Union as some agents reported directly to him.

Secretary Judah Benjamin was his close advisor in intelligence and foreign policy matters. Davis had perhaps the best set of political skills and experience to be a chief executive in his day. He was born in Kentucky and grew up on his brother's cotton plantations in Mississippi and Louisiana. He was a graduate of West Point and was successful troop commander in the Mexican War. Davis served as a US Senator from Mississippi and was the chairman of the Senate Military Affairs Committee. He also was Secretary of War under President Franklin Pierce, 1853-1857.

President Davis was reputed to be abrasive in office (no doubt he was under much stress) and often personally directed military campaigns which irritated his generals. Davis can best be described as his own intelligence officer due to his vast experience. He had a running battle with Beauregard. The only Confederate general who seems to have had his confidence was Robert E. Lee." [13]

General Robert Edward Lee, CSA
Commander of the Army of Northern Virginia

Mills exposes Lee's role: "General Robert E. Lee (1807- 1870) was also a key official in Confederate espionage and had some agents, scouts, and collectors reporting directly to him, especially Colonel Mosby and Major General J. E. B. Stuart. Records indicate Lee was very aware of intelligence operations. He learned earlier in his career the value of good intelligence as he had been very successful in the Mexican War as chief scout for General Winfield Scott and was promoted to brevet colonel.

General Lee can also be described as his own intelligence officer. In addition he had on his staff at least three officers who were involved with intelligence matters, Walter H. Taylor, Charles Marshall, and Charles Venable." [14]

John McNeil and son – Jessie Cunningham McNeil

"After the Confederate Government abolished the Confederate Partisan Rangers Act in 1864, McNeil Rangers were the only officially sanctioned partisan group other than Mosby's Rangers. Like the Thurmond brothers in West Virginia, McNeil's Rangers was a family affair. After John McNeil was mortally wounded in a raid in the fall of 1864. Command passed to his son Jesse Cunningham McNeil." [15]

Notes

1) *The Confederate Secret Service*, by Harold W. Mills, Jr. Convenant Books Inc., Murrels Inlet, SC, 2018, page 15
2) Mills, page 17
3) Mills, page 19
4) Mills, page21
5) Mills, page 22
6) Mills, page 23
7) Mills, page 24
8) Mills, page 25
9) Mills, page 26
10A) Mills, page 27
10B) Mills, page 51
11) Mills, page 36
12) Mills, page 31
13) Mills, page 34
14) Mills, page 35
15) O'Donnell page 279

Chapter Two
Confederate Spies

An introduction to previously unknown Confederate Spies, many of whom were old men, young men, pretty women, older ladies. Black men, white men, many were young boys (the youngest being nine years old). They were of the Jewish faith and of the Christian faith. They were many foreigners too, a French lady from Santo Domingo, a beautiful Irish aristocratic lady, a young British adventurer. And finally there were a few British mercenaries, a real French prince and so on and so forth.

Many were recruited because they would not normally attract much attention. Researchers are shocked at how successful these Confederate spies were. They somehow managed to provide the Confederate Army with accurate information on where the invading union armies were.

While the Confederacy was still in its infancy, the "wild Rose" Rose Greenhow, had set up an all female (all beautiful ladies) spy network in Washington, DC.

The following are a number of previously unknown spies and their stories, I have managed to discover. I believe their sacrifices should be appreciated and their memories preserved for future generations.

Cornelia S. Nichols Cliffe

"The banks of the South's unreconstructed women were further thinned when Mrs Cornelia S. Nichols Cliffe, widow of a Union soldier, but follower of the lost cause, died yesterday. ... It was Mrs. Cliffe who aided only by an old man, faced fire of a federal battery to burn the Nashville bridge and halt temporarily the Union advance on Franklin.

After the battle of Franklin, Mrs. Cliffe was among the first on the field to minister to the wounded Confederates. Her home was converted into a hospital." [1 and 2]

Ananaide Marie Ducayet Simms

"Mrs Ananaide Marie Ducayet Simms expires at Hotel Dieu. With the son who had shared many of her perils as a spy for the Confederates in the civil war, by her bedside. ... Mrs. Simms was a native of New Orleans and a member of a distinguished French family ... when the War Between the States started, Mrs. Simms joined the Confederates as a spy and dispatch carrier and because of her cleverness was only captured twice." [3 and 4]

Lady Eleanor Monteith

Lady Eleanor Monteith was a beautiful Irish aristocrat, who quarreled with her father. She then left Ireland and landed in Canada with her husband: "In 1858 Lady Eleanor's husband died ... the widow and her little girl went to Richmond, VA to live. But there was much work to do — perilous and daring work of all sorts and Lady Eleanor offered her talents to the (Confederate) Secret Service to get letters and dispatches through to Canada and thence England. ... She was well known in Canada and in Great Britain. Easily she established communication with agents there and built up a regular "mail system." She undertook personally the task of carrying dispatches. She did risky errands for the South that no mere man could have achieved. Daily her services grew more valuable to her employers ... the surgeon director general of the Confederacy fell in love with her ... Lady Eleanor promised to marry him. It was said at the time that love for this man, rather than any great sympathy for the Confederate cause induced her. ..."

The Union secret service was long in suspecting Lady Eleanor and still longer in proving she was a Southern spy. But at last her luck deserted her. "She was arrested and was told about the death of the man she loved. It was for him she served the South, and now with his death, the Pinkerton's offered to spare her life and a big salary if she would become a double agent. Charges were dropped, she went to live in a New York hotel, where peep holes in the room above her library allowed the Pinkerton's to hear and see all that Confederate agents visiting her were saying, the mail service between Canada and the South was destroyed and her betrayal did much harm to the Confederate cause." [5 and 6]

Belle Boyd

Unlike most people in this book who remained anonymous during and after the war, this lady spy was famous: "In her engagements with the Southern army she performed many feats of daring. During the battle of Fort Royal she ran across the battlefield (in a dress) under fire from both armies and delivered an important message to General Jackson which saved the bridge from being burned and the officer's army from being surrounded." [7]

Bennet Burleigh (English Soldier of Fortune).

"During the War Between the States, Mr. Burleigh, who was a young and adventure-loving Englishman — a soldier of fortune cast his lot with the side of the Confederacy and fought throughout the

war. During Sherman's march to the sea, he was captured by the federals and transferred to Johnson's Island in Sandusky Bay in Lake Erie. After being imprisoned on light rations for several months (he was starving) and becoming restless and desperate to be free and active again, he planned an escape which became sensational in the annals of the war. The prison at Johnson's Island was thought absolutely escape-proof. As it was almost one mile to the shore, but this did not daunt young Burleigh and two daring companions, and one dark night they ran past the sentries, who were not aware of what was going on until they heard the bodies of the men splash in the water. Burleigh swam to shore and again joined the Confederate ranks. Several months later he was captured and sentenced to be shot as a spy. Never giving up hope, and awaiting his opportunity, one night he overpowered his guard and escaped to again join the ranks of the men in gray and finished the war unscathed." [8]

Clara Gunby

"... Miss Clara Gumby, was a daring, brilliant woman, who also served in the Confederacy as a spy. She made a notable visit in Richmond at one time, securing valuable information. ..." [9 and 10]

Mary Woodman Kimball Rhodes

I was very fortunate to recently find out about a very brave lady, who was a spy and who also had a California connection. She was mainly from the Stockton area (CA), her name was Mary Woodman Kimball Rhodes. I was even more amazed to discover Mary's great-great grand daughter, had done a great job collecting documents which indicated Mary was indeed a spy. She said Mary never talked about her covert activities for fear of having her farm confiscated.

Mary owned property in Stockton, California, and raised money during 1863-1864 for the "Southern Relief Association," to help Confederate prisoners in Union jails. In fact, she raised $70,000 or $1,280,000 in today's money.

The Daily Bee newspaper (Sacramento, CA), said: "But how are we to know that the funds raised by the Southern Relief Association, is devoted to such a purpose? Have we any assurance that the money is not smuggled into Dixie and there used by the rebels in arm."

In fact, the provost marshal of the middle district of California, whose duties include finding spies, wanted Mary arrested, General Wright, refused to have her arrested. He was the commanding General of California (derisively called granny Wright by the unionist press). Mary immediately left and continued her activities, she was indeed a clever operative.

As a result, the Secretary of War issued an arrest warrant for her saying: "She is a rebel and emissary (spy or secret agent) bitterly hostile to the government and devoting herself to aid the rebels and their cause and is dangerous to be at large. She is over 50 years of age and her family are all in the rebel service. You will have diligent search made for her and if found placed under arrest, guards allowing no communications any person and have her effects seized and herself searched."

I am guessing she worked for General Lee's intelligence network. She never spoke of her activities and it is not known if the Provost Marshall's files on her survived. Mary was never caught and after the war in 1866, she received a very touching letter from Robert E. Lee himself, praising her service to the cause and wishing her well in her return to California.

This heroine of the Confederate Secret Service, tragically lost all of her three sons fighting for the cause, the sadness shows in her photograph. It is time for her to be properly honored and the memory of her deeds preserved. [11, 12 and 13]

John W. Kline

"Though but a boy, Mr. Kline served the Confederacy as a spy under Johnston during the siege, and his very youth made him a valuable asset to the Secret Service." [14 and 15]

John C. Laws

"John C. Laws, scout for General Nathan Bedford Forrest during the War Between the States, died last night at his home here. He was 88. Too young to enlist as a soldier. Laws served the Confederacy as a scout, his youth enabling him to slip through federal lines and obtain military information." [16 and 17]

Ted Boyias

John Harrison Suratt

"John Harrison Suratt, the last survivor of the corps of alleged conspirators tried for implication in the plot to assassinate Abraham Lincoln, died here today. In the civil war he served in the Confederate Secret Service. When he heard that a warrant had been issued for him, he fled from New York to Canada. He was acquitted after being brought back for trial and came to Baltimore." [18 and 19]

Colonel Henry J. Leovy

Was special commissioner to Secretary of State, Judah P. Benjamin: "He also oversaw the suppression of treason against the Confederacy. Special commissioners who investigated and arrested those disloyal to the government reported to Benjamin. For example, Col. Henry J. Leovy, a close friend of Benjamin from New Orleans, served as military commissioner in southwest Virginia. His job was ferreting out traitors."

The Secretary of State Benjamin had his very own intelligence network, which he financed with his own money. [20]

Major Alexander "Alex" Hart

Another Jewish officer who became a counterspy: "Hart was wounded again at Gettysburg by a gunshot to his left hand. He spent the rest of the summer of 1863 recuperating. In November he was certified as permanently disabled and assigned to the department of Henrico (Richmond) under Brig. General John H. Winder (Provost Marshall of Richmond) whose duties were to hunt down spies, traitors and deserters." [21]

Lieutenant Colonel William Mallory Levy

Levy was an officer and a Jewish spy: "On June 18, Magruder (Colonel John Bankhead Magruder) sent Captain Levy under a flag of truce to Fort Monroe, and he returned with the intelligence that an expedition of some magnitude was underway, prompting Magruder to move back to Yorktown." [22]

Captain H. Kennedy

"This was the general situation when Captain H. Kennedy CSA, landed at San Francisco, on July 7, 1864. Emerging from obscurity for a moment and standing in the light. He was an obscure person, so obscure that today we do not even know what given name was represented by the initial letter H. In the records of the war, he is simply H. Kennedy, Captain CSA. We may surmise he was a Texan, solely because he started his adventures from Texas, and returned to Texas upon completion of his dangerous mission. We may surmise too that he was an experienced frontiersman and a soldier of proven courage and ability; otherwise he would never have been charged with the mission of a Confederate agent in California." [23]

Antonia Ford Willard

"She was a wealthy lady, who volunteered to become a Confederate secret service agent. Her brother was one of Mosby's partisan rangers: Her tactics was to circulate among union officers and gather valuable intelligence on troop strengths and movements." [24]

She helped Stuart at the battle of First Manassas, and Mosby in his capture of General Stoughton in his bed. In 1863 she got arrested for spying, luckily she landed in jail and was not hanged. She took the oath of allegiance and married Union Major Joseph C. Willard who was one of her jailers. They later operated together the famous Willard Hotel. [24]

Major General J. E. B. Stuart

J. E. B. Stuart was Robert E. Lee's spymaster, he was: "The senior Cavalry commander for the Army of Northern Virginia, and as such, he worked closely with his commander Robert E. Lee. Stuart led aggressive scouting missions to know where the enemy was and to help General Lee avoid surprise." [25]

Ted Boyias

Colonel John Singleton Mosby

As a spymaster himself, Mosby ably ran not one, but actually two intelligence spy networks for his boss general J. E. B. Stuart: "He proved himself a premier intelligence officer, combining the highest skill." [26]

Mosby would emerge not only as a guerrilla leader who pioneered a new form of warfare but also as a master spy.

Captain Benjamin Franklin Stringfellow

Colonel Mills, a former Intelligence Officer, and author of a book on the Confederate Secret Service, considers Stringfellow to be one of J. E. B. Stuart's best agents: "Benjamin Franklin Stringfellow, he posed as a dentist's assistant in union occupied Alexandria Virginia and sent regular reports of union troop movements." [27]

However, there seems to be some folks who may dispute the claim of his being one of the best of Stuart's agents: "Fresh off their victory against Hunter, Mosby sought to vanquish Cole and his cavalry once and for all. An opportunity to destroy their nemesis presented itself in the form of ninety-four pound Frank Stringfellow. The twenty-something scout and favorite of J. E. B. Stuart claimed to have disguised himself as a Yankee colonel and had dinner with Union General John Sedgwick, he later spied for the South undercover as a dental assistant in Alexandria, where he was closer to his beautiful fiancée Emma Green. His narrow escapes and derring-do were legendary and sometimes sounded too good to be true, because they were. As Mosby remembered, "He was a brave soldier, but a great liar." He was also an elite agent in the Confederate Secret Service."

Lou Eleanor Dorsey Ewing

There was a pretty young lady in Missouri who dared to serve her country and her people during the bloody War Between the States. She describes in her own words what she did: "I feel much like a veteran myself. No fault of mine that I did not shoulder a musket. Many nights with windows heavily draped, I moulded bullets, made clothing, knapsacks, haversacks, tents — smuggled hundreds of meals for my brother's recruits. Would many days ride 40 to 50 miles begging for money, clothing for our prisoners (Confederates). Then run the gauntlet. ..."

Most riders today can barely ride five miles, and she rode mostly at night accompanied only by a companion, through yankee and red leg patrols (Union Guerrilla fighters who wore red leather boots). She carried messages which could have easily gotten her hanged if discovered. It really was like running a gauntlet. Her brother Caleb was a Colonel in General Sterling Prices' army. There is a coded letter from her brother that has survived, where he is talking about "stock" cattle, but he is really referring to recruits." [30]

A second coded letter from her Cousin Geo. B. Clarke, refers to: "Your messages to cousin Caleb (her brother), per flag of truce, already en route ... Uncle Sterling (General Sterling Price), is about to attempt you a visit. May the kind hearted old gentleman have a pleasant journey." [31]

Lou had a total of 40 cousins who fought for the South. One of them was cousin Samuel Dorsey who owned the Beauvoir Estate and its plantation in Biloxi, Mississippi. After his death, Samuels' widow bequeathed this property to President Jeff Davis.

Lou is one of a handful of Confederate lady Secret Service Agents with a California connection. Her bravery and the risks she took should be made known and the memory of this brave lady must be preserved. [28, 29, 30 and 31]

Captain Thomas Jordan

"The man who enlisted Rose Greenhow, as a spy was Captain Thomas Jordan, an assistant quartermaster of the War Department staff. Of the scores of US Army officers, who gave up their commissions and went to the South, Jordan was one of the very last to leave Washington. During the interim, Jordan had been very aggressive in completing his arraignments for what was almost certainly be the Confederacy's first spy ring, with none other than Rose Greenhow as its operating head. What made this spy network unique was that it was composed of women." [32]

Thomas Nelson Conrad

Conrad set up a Confederate spy network in Washington, DC, right under federal spy chief Lafayette's Baker's nose: "Colonel Lafayette Baker had a reputation for utter ruthlessness. During his regime, citizens disappear from their homes in the night; so many prisoners were held, often without charges. To escape the clutches of Lafayette Baker, Thomas Conrad devised an elaborate scheme. Shortly after he took up residence in Washington, Conrad arranged to have a Confederate enlisted man to pretend to desert, make his way to Washington and present himself to Baker as an embittered Southerner who desired to work for the union as a counterespionage agent. His name was Edward Norton." [33]

Edward Norton

Conrad the Confederate spymaster describes his recruit, Edward Norton: "He was a brave young fellow with no end of brass and self assurance." Incredibly Baker took the bait, and according to Conrad, the: "Up shot of it all was that Norton received an appointment as one of Colonel Baker's most trusted detectives." [34]

"Conrad's success in placing his double agent on Baker's force undoubtedly saved his own life. Sometime in mid-1863, Norton warned Conrad that Baker was in pursuit of him, assigning Norton to run affairs in his absence, Conrad fled from Washington, and less than an hour after Conrad's departure, Baker's men raided the Van Ness mansion, but came away empty-handed." [35]

(No first name Skillman)
Skillman, a Confederate spy and courier was bushwhacked and killed by General Carleton's scouts (Californians), on the Texas border (Coleman scouts were a famous group of scouts who were active in the Kentucky-Tennessee regions, numbering more than 100 troopers. Skillman was one of these Coleman scouts.) [36]

Henry Thomas Harrison — (no first name Schreiber)
Two great scouts who provided accurate information to General Longstreet as to the location of the Union army at Gettysburg. Raphael J. Moses, the Confederate Army's most competent commissary officer supplied food, clothes for the army. ... Moses was privy to all of the top level discussions, even those that involving civilian spies, Harrison and Schreiber, who gave Lee the exact position of the Union army, but Lee distrusted the men and refused to rely on their reports, which turned out to be true." [37 and 38]

(No first name) Jeffries
Jeffries was a double agent working for the Yankees: "Here is an example of how the (US) army used a man that had been arrested (a Southerner).

At some point after his release from arrest, military authorities in the Department of Ohio recruited Jeffries to be a spy. ... Jeffries later on is on the payroll of the detective corps of the Cincinnati Post Command. ... While working on that force he infiltrated the Confederate network operating there and in Northern Kentucky. But Confederate agents working for Captain Thomas Henry Hines, one of the Confederate government's leading secret agents, discovered his identity as an army spy. Hines' men seized him and executed him in the woods near Flat Rock, Kentucky, in January 1865." [39]

Captain Thomas Hines

Hines is often referred to as: The most competently dangerous man in the Confederacy. A very dangerous 23 year old guerrilla fighter. A Confederate spy who was appointed military leader of the Northwest (today known as Midwest), but which also included the northeastern United States as well as the border states areas of Kentucky and Missouri. "In 1864 the *New York Times* hinted it had been a vast Confederate plan to spread a siege of terror from Maine to Minnesota. This claim was only partially true, the objective was not just to make raids on northern cities — the overthrow of the United States government by revolution was the principal goal of the conspiracy ... the men were young and handsome, mostly hard-bitten veterans of General John Hunt Morgan's command, "the rebel raider" as the north knew him." [40]

Philip Henson

Double agent and notorious traitor to his Southern roots. Henson worked for Ulysses S. Grant's spy-chief, who was Brigadier General Grenville M. Dodge: "His agents were soldier scouts, unionists living in Confederate areas, and women couriers. Dodge financed his spying by selling confiscated cotton. None of these people were Pinkertons (detectives), but for Dodge his ace agent was Philip Henson, described as, "probably the ablest man in our service." Henson possessed many attributes that made him ideal spy material. He was a native Southerner and had no need to fake the accent of the region. He fooled General Leonidas Polk, when Henson walked into Polk's headquarters and offered his services and some information. Polk foolishly hired this federal spy to work for his spy network. But he was not the only one, three other generals were conned by Henson and hired him too, they were David Ruggles, Samuel Gholson, and Samuel Ferguson.

Henson was on a roll, but his luck ran out when he was: "Sent to spy on the activities of the Confederacy's ferocious Cavalryman, Nathan Bedford Forrest. Henson was arrested by Forrest's men." [41]

Henson rotted in solitary confinement, he may have fooled all of the other generals but he didn't fool Forrest who considered him a traitor. Later on when Forrest found out about his activities Forrest lamented that he had not hanged the Yankees' most dangerous spy.

Nancy C. Hart

Nancy C. Hart, a Confederate guide and spy, was also a member of the Mocasin Rangers, a notorious band of West Virginia bushwackers. When she was arrested, she conned the guard to let her use his loaded rifle as a prop when she was having her mugshot taken. She then shot him through the heart and in a flash she escaped jumping out of a window. Two weeks later, she returned to guide the 22nd Virginia Cavalry, helping them to capture all of her Union enemies without a fight. [42]

Jacob Bloomstein

Jewish Confederates spy who was: "… arrested in May of 1863 as a spy and for smuggling goods through the lines to the Confederate army. He was later released by Governor Johnson." [43]

Eugenia Phillips

There were some Jewish Confederate spies who were women: "Eugenia Phillips was born in Charleston in 1819. A high-spirited woman, she married a successful lawyer, Philip Phillips. They moved to Washington, DC, when Mr Phillips was elected to congress. Mrs Phillips was arrested twice by Union authorities, first in Washington for spying and then in New Orleans for mocking Union soldiers. Mary Chestnut referred to her and fellow spy Rose Greenhow as "Saints and martyrs and patriots." After being imprisoned along with her children and husband for three weeks, she was released. They could find no evidence against her. The story was later widely circulated that Eugenia brought a message in code from Rose Greenhow in a ball of yarn and delivered it to Jefferson Davis." [44, 45, 46]

William Ledbetter- Sam Davis

"He was one of the states most prominent Confederates having commanded the Rutherford Rifles, Company I, First Regiment, composed of 150 picked men, Sam Davis was a member of this company and it is thought Captain Ledbetter had knowledge of some of secret information bravos possessed as to how he obtained the federal plans and because of this refusal to reveal the traitor in the federal ranks Davis was hanged at Pulaski." [47]

Woodson Worth Moffett

"During the civil war years, in spite of his immature years, he was a member of a Mississippi regiment. A large part of his service was running down renegades and deserters." [48] [49]

Here is a partial list of prisoners being released after taking the oath, from the Old Capitol prison in Washington, DC. These were prisoners they did not have enough evidence to hold them.

F. M. Ellis, December 20, 1861, employed in Secret Service of Gen. McClellan and communicating information to the rebels."Ellis was a double agent who while spying for US General McClellan, was giving information to the rebels." [50]

Henry A. Stewart. December 12, 1861.
Employed by J. P. Benjamin, rebel Secretary of War. In other words, Stewart was a Confederate spy, paid by Judah P. Benjamin out of his own pocket. [51]

James Potter, January 30, 1862, for spying and shooting at Union pickets. [51A]

Josiah E. Bailey, February 1, 1862, Spy (rebel officer found in Washington in citizen's clothes). [52]

Francis A. Dickens, Spy. [53]

M. T. Walworth – Mrs. Morris
M. T. Walworth, spy, connected with Mrs. Morris and William T. Smithson; Mrs Morris and Smith, connected with Walworth, sent to Washington by Gen. Johnston. Mrs. Augusta H. Morris. (same Mrs. Morris) Spy. [54]

Thomas J. Magruder, February 11, 1862, Spy. [55]

Thomas Haycock, February 13, 1862, Spy. [56]

Warren Curtis, February 13, 1862, Spy, prowling about Union camps. [57]

William P. Bryan, February 21, 1862. Spy and unquestionably employed by the rebel government." [58]

E. Pliny Bryan. Spy, February 21, 1862, belongs to the rebel signal corps." [59]

What this list shows is the extent of the activities of the Confederate Secret Service, how widespread they were, and the amazing bravery of these patriotic spies. Unfortunately, many were tried and convicted after being tortured by people like Lafayette Baker self proclaimed head of the federal secret service. They were hanged without a trial, never to be heard of again.

"The Rambler (author), finds it necessary to leave the remainder of the list for another ramble. The whole list would make this story too long. But I have room for an observation or two. You see that Pliny Bryan was charged with being a spy. Captain Bryan's home was Bryan Hall. He was not on a spying trip, but on furlough to visit his mother." [60]

Major General Benjamin Franklin Cheatham

"This patriot was a California Gold Miner, who lived in Stockton Northern California before the war." Cheatham was also instrumental in founding a legendary group of scouts, the Coleman Scouts. "Among the most noted bands of Confederate scouts was one organized by General Cheatham over which one Henry B. Shaw was put in command." [61 and 62]

Colonel J. Stoddard Johnston

"As the war went on, each commanding general relied on his own spies and the scouts of his Cavalry leader. Colonel J. Stoddard Johnston was a nephew of Albert Sidney Johnston and served. as a spy on General Bragg's staff from Stone's river to Chattanooga, all through this important campaign he had charge of the secret-service orders and reports. He has related how he always utilized soldiers of known intelligence, honor, and daring, as spies, without extra compensation, and employed the Cavalry of Wheeler, Morgan and Forrest as scouts." [63]

Vespasian Chance Chancellor

"The scouts were the real eyes and ears of the army. From the very beginning of the war the Confederate Cavalry was much used for scouting purposes, even at the time when federal commanders were still chiefly dependent upon civilian spies, detectives, and deserters for information as to their opponents strength and movements, they saw the folly of this, after much disastrous experience, and came to rely like Confederates on keen-witted cavalrymen. The true scout must be an innate lover of adventure, with the sharpest of eyesight and undaunted courage. Such was Vespasian Chancellor, one of the most successful scouts in General J. E. B. Stuart's Cavalry command. He was directly attached to the General's headquarters." [64]

Henry B. Shaw

As mentioned previously: "Among the most noted bands of Confederate scouts was one organized by General Cheatham, over which one Henry B. Shaw was put in command. Shaw, who had been a clerk

on a steamboat plying between Nashville and New Orleans, had an accurate knowledge of middle Tennessee, which in the summer of 1863 was in the hands of the federal army, owing to Bragg's retreat from Tullahoma. He assumed the disguise of an itinerant doctor while in the federal lines, and called himself Dr. C. E. Coleman. In the Confederate army he was known as Captain C. E. Coleman, commander of General Bragg's private scouts. The scouts dressed as Confederate soldiers, so that in case of capture they would not be treated as spies. Nevertheless, the information they carried was usually put into cipher.

Shaw was finally captured and sent to Johnson's Island. The command of the famous scouts devolved upon Alexander Greg's, who continued to sign dispatches, "C. E. Coleman," and the federal authorities never knew the original leader of the daring band was in safe-keeping in Sandusky Bay." (prison) [65]

Alexander Gregg

When Henry B. Shaw, the leader of the famous Coleman scouts was arrested, his command was given to Alexander Gregg. Gregg continued to sign his dispatches C E. Coleman, as if Shaw was still running the Coleman Scouts. Thus, the federals had no idea the man they had in jail in Sandusky Bay, was the leader of the famous Coleman Scouts. [66]

Colonel Vincent Marmaduke

"Colonel Vincent Marmaduke of St. Louis, died here today, age 73. He was a Confederate and as a member of the Knights of the Golden Circle during the civil war was arrested on a trip to Chicago. He was a son of John F. Marmaduke one of the early Missouri governors and his brother was governor of Missouri after the war." He was most likely a spy. [67 and 68]

Captain J. G. Foreacre

"A few moments after General … fell (he was waving a flag to encourage his men during the battle of first Manassas July 21, 1861) when he was shot dead. … Captain (Foreacre) was most seriously wounded, but soon the deadly ball he carried so poisoned his life that he was compelled to go into home service and was the first Provost Marshall of Atlanta from 1862 to 1865." [69 and 70]

(Provost Marshall's duties included ferreting out traitors, deserters-being a counter spy.)

Colonel Ed C. Wilson [71 and 72]

Sam Alexander-Syd Ferguson-Cab Maddox-Lewis "the terrible" Powell

This is a rare description of an engagement of these four scouts of Colonel Mosby's command: "Another storm of lead flew by. The rangers closed in within thirty yards, their revolvers peppering away at the two.

Ted Boyias

From the throng of Confederates four men broke out to pursue Blazer and pancake (nickname). They were "the best soldiers in Mosby's command" Sam Alexander, Syd Ferguson, Cab Maddox and Lewis the "Terrible" Powell. Riding "on one of the fastest and fleetest and hardiest animal in the battalion," Ferguson gained on Blazer and pancake. "I am going to get out of this, "muttered pancake as he spurred his horse and bolted forward.

"The hunters (union Blazer scouts) had become the hunted — on one of the countless engagements involving irregulars in a largely shadow war that raged behind the scenes of the great battles of the civil war." [73] We were never told what happened next.

John C. Courtney

"Major Courtney was a native of Virginia, early in life he entered the field of telegraphy, and during the civil war was closely associated with Generals Lee, Beauregard and Johnston, in establishing communication between the Confederate armies and headquarters. He delivered to General Beauregard the first news of General Lee's surrender and also bore to president Jefferson Davis the dispatch from General Breckinridge announcing the assassination of President Lincoln.

Subsequently he was taken to Washington to corroborate this dispatch before the court-martial engaged in the investigation of Lincoln's assassination." [74 and 75]

Colonel Alfred Jones

Liam Opie says the following about his ancestor: "My five (times) great uncle. Originally an aide-de-camp to General Sterling Price 1861. He later went to Canada (many Confederate spies lived there). After being released from union captivity, before being extradited to the United States by the British in June of 1865, for his involvement in the yellow fever plot. Was nearly executed but had his life spared." [76]

James Fowle

"A spy that had to testify before congress in regards to the Lincoln assasination." [77]

Nicholas J. Watkins

"… Was appointed as a member of the signal department of the Confederate army." [78 and 79]

Asbury Harpending

"Asbury was one of the leaders of the Knights of the Golden Circle, one of the 30 wealthy San Franciscans — who each commanded 100 soldiers, whom they supported financially. These fighting men were unfortunately, mostly mercenaries, adventurers and therefore, unreliable. When the Comstock Lode of silver was discovered they ran to Virginia City, Nevada to get rich.

Asbury made a fatal mistake when he financed a privateer ship (the blockade runner ship called the *Chapman*). This was done in San Francisco right under the federal's noses. Asbury didn't personally vet or hire the crew himself. As a result, his friends hired a young loudmouth criminal, who blew the whole operation, and nearly got Asbury hanged." [80]

Thurmond Brothers — Notorious West Virginia Bushwackers

"The Thurmonds ardently supported the Confederate cause and also owned enslaved peoples. Brothers Phillip and William Thurmond founded Thurmond's rangers, two companies of partisans from local clans in the area, forty-two-year-old William would never surrender or take the oath of allegiance even after the war ended. In West Virginia, chaos and lawlessness reigned, and the Thurmonds' thrived … in the heart of Appalachia where feuds among clans such as the Hatfields and McCoys were woven into the culture, the bonds of blood and friendship ran deep and reinforced their allegiance to the Confederate cause. Composed of many outlaws and deserters, paramilitary groups such as the Thurmonds, often derisively referred to as "bushwhackers" by the union, terrorized or protected the civilians around them depending on their loyalties. They were knights of the ravines and caves. … Terror to the country, noted for deeds of daring behind rocks, lying behind logs like other venomous reptiles, only more certain death when they drew a bead on a man, besides blocking the roads in every possible way, annoying the advance guard and prisoners, they would lurk along the rear of a column and shoot footsore, sick, exhausted, soldiers and helpless soldiers who fell easy prey to these fiendish, barbarous bushwackers, one union officer recalled." (A form of mountain fighting developed from earlier wars against the Indians, from Tory against Patriot feuds during the American revolution, and from family feuds later on. Shooting from behind trees and logs was common, as well as shooting someone in the back. Sometimes it is referred as fighting mountain way).

"… Thurmond's rangers conducted guerrilla warfare by hiding in safe houses and rallying at a designated point to conduct raids on federal outposts and units, after which they would melt back into the civilian population to engage in farming … intelligence played a vital role. The Thurmond brothers established a series of spies and couriers who would relay union movements so they could pounce on federal weak points." [81 and 82]

Sarah Slater

Her nickname was the "French woman," she may have been French or Cajun: "The French woman "one of the South's couriers and spies trusted with the most important dispatches." [83]

In conclusion: "The guerrillas and bushwackers gave no quarter; they regularly executed captured scouts. A war of annihilation raged in Appalachia."

Notes

1) Title: Woman who braved fire of Union battery dies. *Chattanooga Times* (newspaper), Franklin Tenn., Dec. 11, 1928
2) Book: *A Self - Professed Confederate Obituaries and U.S. Newspaper Mentions* By Janet Lindeman Fiore, Volume 1, page 33.
3) Title: Noted Woman Spy of the Confederacy Dies in N. O. (New Orleans), *The New Orleans Item* (newspaper) *The Daily Arkansas Gazette* (newspaper) Little Rock, Arkansas, 3 Nov. 1917- page 16
4) Ibid Fiore, page 150, Vol. 1
5) *Tulsa Morning Times* (newspaper), Tulsa Oklahoma, Mar., 21, 1918. Title: Stories of Spies, by Albert Payson Terhune.
6) Ibid Fiore, page 115, Vol. 1
7) *Evansville Courier & Press* (newspaper), Evansville Indiana, June 17, 1900, p. 16. Title: Death of Belle Boyd. The Famous Spy Who Served the Confederacy.
8) Title: War Hero Has a Son in Arkansas. *Daily Arkansas Gazette* (newspaper) Little Rock Arkansas, 19 June 1914, p. 1.
9) *The Atlanta Constitution* (newspaper). Atlanta, GA, 24 March, 1901, p. 23.
10) Ibid Fiore page 67, Vol. 1.
11) *The Daily Bee* (newspaper), Sacramento CA, March 5, 1864.
12) Telegram from Secretary of War from Washington, DC, March 28, 1864.
13) Entire typewritten letter of Robert E. Lee, 15 March 1866, Lexington Virginia.
14) *Vicksburg Evening Post* (newspaper), Vicksburg, MS, 8 July 1907 -p.6
15) Ibid. Fiore, page 94, Vol. 1.
16) Title: John C. Laws, 88, dies; Was a Scout for Forrest, *The Atlanta Constitution* (newspaper), Atlanta Georgia, 4 Dec 1937, p. 4.
17) Ibid Fiore, page 97, Vol. 1.
18) *Arizona Daily Star* (newspaper) 22 April, 1916- page 3.
19) Ibid Fiori, page 159, Vol. 1.
20) Book: Rosen, Robert N. (2000). *The Jewish Confederates*, University of South Carolina Press, Columbia, South Carolina, pages 80 -81.
21) Ibid, Rosen, page 103.
22) Ibid pages 105- 106.

23) Book: *California Knights of the Golden Circle*, by Ted Boyias, The Scuppernong Press, Wake Forest, NC, 2023, page 1.
24) Book: *By Harold W, Mills Jr.*, Covenant Books, Inc, 2018, Murrells Inlet, SC, 29576, page 49.
25) Ibid Mills, page 29.
26) Book: *Generals in Gray*, by Ezra J. Warner, Louisiana State University Press, Baton Rouge and London 1959, page 296.
27) Ibid Mills, page 530.
28) Application for membership in UDC, California
29) Caleb's coded letter to Lou
30) Letter from cousin Geo. B. Clarke to Lou, September 19, 1864.
31) Sources anonymous unpublished manuscripts.
32) Davis William C. Book: *Spies, Scouts, and Raiders, Irregular Operations During the Civil War*, Alexandria, Virginia. 1985, page 24.
33) Davis, 1985, pages 56-57
34) Ibid Davis
35) Ibid Davis
36) Hunt, 1951/ 2004, page 76
37) Rosen, page 130
38) Moses, Raphael J., Book: *Last Order of the Lost Cause: The Civil War Memoirs of a Jewish Family From the Old South*, Univ. Press of America, 1995.
39) Boyias 2023, page 101.
40) Horan, 1960, *The Fairfax Press*, MCMLIV, page 3.
41) Davis, 1985, page 78.
42) Boyias, page 145.
43) Boyias, 2023, page 145
44) Rosen, page 282.
45) Manuscript: Phillips Diary, 38. Mrs. Phillips: *A Southern Woman's Story of Her imprisonment in 1861 and 1862* Library of Congress manuscript Division 4.
46) *Leaf - Chronicle*, Clarksville, TN, 16 July 1906, page 6.
47) Fiore page 99, Vol. 2.
48) *The Greenwood Commonwealth* (newspaper), Greenwood MS, 14 April 1937- page 1.
49) Fiore, page 119, vol. 2
50) Title: Rambler (author's pseudonym) *The Sunday Star* (newspaper) Washington, DC, Oct 24, 1926, page 3.
51) *The Star* newspaper: Tuesday, July 23, 1861. Washington DC

52) Ibid.
53) Ibid.
54) Ibid.
55) Ibid.
56) Ibid.
57) Ibid.
58) Ibid.
59) Ibid.
60) Ibid.
61) Boyias, page 3.
62) *Soldier Life and the Secret Service*, Editor-in-Chief Francis Trevelyan Miller, Castle Books, New York, 1957, page 292.
63) Ibid Miller, page 292.
64) Ibid Miller, page 295
65) Ibid. Miller. Page 292
66) Ibid Miller page. 292
67) Title: Death of Colonel Vincent Marmaduke. *The San Francisco Examiner*, San Francisco, CA, page 7.
68) Fiore, page 105, Vol. 1.
69) *Atlanta Semi-Weekly Journal*, Atlanta Georgia, 17 July 1902, page 8.
70) Fiore, page 54, Vol. 2.
71) Title of Obituary: Rites Today For Spy For General Lee.
Fort Worth Star-Telegram, Fort Worth Texas, 8 Nov 1933- page 11.
72) Fiore, page 180, vol. 1.
73) Book: *The Unvanquished-The Untold Story of Lincoln's Special Forces*, Atlantic Monthly Press, New York, 2024, page XIV. By Patrick K. O'Donnell.
74) *The Sun* (newspaper), Baltimore Maryland, 14 July 1899- page 2.
75) Fiore, page 33, vol. 2.
76) Unpublished Manuscript by Liam Opie
77) Ibid Opie.
78) Title: Mr. N. J. Watkins Dead, *The Washington Post* (newspaper), Washington, DC, 4 Mar 1908- page 4.
79) Fiore, page 174, vol. 1.
80) Ibid O'Donnell, pages 61-62.
81) Ibid O'Donnell, page 15.
82) O'Donnell page 355
83) O'Donnell page 355

Chapter Three
Scouts

An Introduction

One must never underestimate the role of the scouts during the War Between the States, the following clearly shows this: "As the war went on, each commanding general relied upon his own spies and the scouts of his cavalry leader. Colonel J. Stoddard Johnston was a nephew of Albert Sidney Johnston and served on General Bragg's staff from Stones River to Chattanooga. All through this important campaign he had charge of the Secret Service Orders and reports. He has related how he always utilized soldiers of known intelligence, honor, and daring as spies, without extra compensation and employed the cavalrymen of Wheeler, Morgan and Forrest as scouts. It was the same with Lee and the commanders in the Trans-Mississippi department.

In Stonewall Jackson's 1862 campaign against Banks, Fremont and Shields in the Valley of Virginia, the Federal forces were defeated within a month, in five battles by an army the aggregated one fifth of their total though divided numbers. This great achievement must not be attributed entirely to the genius of Jackson and the valor of his army. A part of the glory must be to the unknown daring spies and faithful scouts of Ashby's Cavalry, who were darting day and night, in all directions, their unerring information enabled Jackson to strike and invariably escape. On the other hand, the federal generals had no such means of gathering information. And they seem never to have been protected from surprise or advised of Jackson's movements." [1]

The first commander of the Jessie Scouts (union) describes his outfit by saying: "A scout is a man who finds out how far the enemy's pickets extend, the position and strength of the enemy, and also ascertains such general facts as may be useful in the conduct of war. There are no rules for the operation of scouts. They are generally independent and have little if any organization; they are in fact spies. You can not call us fellows anything less than spies, but scout is a more respectable name. Scouts are armed and either fight or surrender, according to the chances. I have often been asked what was the business of the scout; and the best answer I ever gave was, that it is his business to find out other men's business. The line between scout and spy is blurred." ²

I totally agree with his assessment, scouts are spies indeed.

The following are stories of scouts nobody has ever heard of:

Jim. P. Athey

"The following is from Monday's *Fort Scott Tribune* and tells a bit of history of the late J. P. Athey that is doubtless unknown to many of his friends in this county. There is something remarkable in the life of J. P. Athey, who committed suicide a week ago today at his home in Coffeville. During the war he was a scout in the Confederate Army and served with considerable distinction. He was all through the South and was in many bad fights in Virginia. After the war he didn't say much about his participation in the Confederate army, and I doubt if there were half a dozen people in the city who knew that he was a Confederate soldier." 3 and 4

There is only one incident of his on record, where he happened to spy a 2,500 head herd of cattle the yanks were quietly moving through Confederate lines. Athey saw them and none of the federals got their steaks that night, but the hungry Confederates did.

William Mercer Buck

"Confederate army veteran believed to be Oklahoma's sole survivor of the South's civil war army, died here Monday night at the age of 98. He was General William Mercer Buck who received his high rank at the 1948 encampment in Chattanooga. He served in the war as a scout." 5 and 6

Colonel J. Givens Craddock

"Seventy-four years old: a pensioner of the Mexican War: A scout who served the Confederacy in the red days from '61 to '65…." 7 and 8

James E. Hutchins. (16 year old scout)

"Mr. Hutchins joined the Confederate Army at the age of 16 and was a member of the Whitaker's Scouts of Mississippi, being the last survivor of that group. He saw active service with General Lee in Virginia." 9 and 10

Colonel George D. Shaborne

"Col. George D. Shaborne for many years prominent in San Francisco legal circles and Chief of Scouts in the Confederate Army in the civil war, died here today." [11 and 12]

Andrew Jackson Moses, Jr.

He was a 16-year-old Jewish scout. He ran away from school twice, first at 14, later on again at 16 to join the Confederate army: "Later he served as a scout and at war's end, he participated in the courageous defense of Sumter against a unit of Sherman's Army, Potter's raiders."

We are lucky to have some surviving stories about Jack: "Jack's widow Adele, in a 1919 application for a pension, further describes some of these events, she states "on a scouting expedition with Charley Jones, during Potter's raid, when the latter killed a Union soldier, both were eagerly sought for by the federal troops and had a price set on theirs heads."

As my mother, Helen Moses Regenstein Jack's granddaughter, has written: "Many times my father told me the story of how the Yankees surrounded the house and told Jack's mother, Danae Octavia, that they would: "catch that son of yours and hang him from the highest tree in the front yard," and she answered: 'You 'll have to catch him first.'" [13]

Berry H. Binford

"Berry H. Binford, who was the youngest soldier in the Confederate Army, died yesterday. His father, Dr. Binford was a surgeon in the Confederate Army, the boy was 9 years old, struck out to find his father, and reported to Gen. Wheeler, who took him for a federal spy sent by some of the Union people. The general kept an eye on the little chap and finally turned him over to Col. Josiah Patterson, who knew Dr. Binford and at once assumed the care of the boy. It is stated young Binford and another boy, not much older, undertook to do a little special service once they went out between the lines, somewhere up North Alabama. They threw up some breastworks and awaited the advance of the federals. The column came in sight and the boys opened fire as if backed by an army, the boys held the fort a whole day and when night came on they scampered off and rejoined their command several miles away." [14 and 15]

John Devoti

"When the civil war broke out Mr. Devoti entered the Confederate ranks and was made a special scout under Simon Bolivar Buckner, famous Kentucky General. He served from the beginning to the end of the grim conflict being captured on one occasion and serving several months in prison. His career as a scout was indeed remarkable. He saw Gen. Morgan shot down at Greenville, John Devoti, was distinguished for his bravery, coolness, and strategy. He rendered invaluable service to the Confederacy." [16 and 17]

Jasper Cope Lewis

"He volunteered at the beginning of the war in Captain Richard's company … and for the first year did scout duty. Then he was assigned to Rosser's brigade. One horse was shot under him at Orange and another at Winchester. Mr. Lewis was wounded five times, twice seriously." [18 and 19]

Captain Claiborne Henderson McAlpine

"At the outbreak of the civil war, he joined a company of Arkansas Scouts." [20 and 21]

Captain J. J. Montgomery

"Captain Montgomery was a native of Giles county, and joined the Southern army at the breaking out of the war. His adventurous disposition and courage led him in 1862 to join the scouts, properly designated: "the eyes of the army." During his career in the service he was captured a number of times and placed in prison. He was at various intervals an inmate of camp Douglas IL, Camp Morton, IN, and other prisons. However, he always managed to escape. Gen. Wheeler gave him, in 1864 a pass, a pass which showed in what confidence he was held by the Southern leaders, it reads: "All guards will pass J. J. Montgomery, Lowry's Scouts." [22 and 23]

Major Rufus M. Tankesley

"Major Tankesley had a brilliant war record. He was a brave and faithful soldier and was loved by every man under his command. He was one of the most reliable scouts in the Army of Tennessee. He was a personal friend of Gen. Bate deceased, and was pronounced dead by him and others to have been one of the best soldiers in the Confederate army." [24 and 25]

Notes

1) Francis Trevelyan Miller, pages 291-292.
2) Title of article: Adventures of Captain Carpenter, *Richmond Weekly Palladium*, February 13, 1863, page 1.
3) *The Evening Star,* (newspaper), Independence Kansas, 19 Mar, 1910 Page 6.
4) Fiore, page 4, Vol. 1.
5) *The Ponca City News* (newspaper), 11 July 1950, page 1.
6) Fiore, page 22, Vol. 1.
7) Title: Veteran of two wars — interesting career of Col. J. Givens Craddock of Kentucky, *The Kansas City Time*, (newspaper),Kansas City MO, 30 March 1900 Page 8.
8) Fiore, page 37, Vol.1
9) Title: Hutchins Rites at Utica Today, *Clarion Ledger* (newspaper), Jackson Mississippi, 26 July 1939, page 3.
10) Fiore, page 83, vol.1.
11)Title: Confederate Vet Dies. *Pine Bluff Daily Graphic* (newspaper), Pine Bluff AR, 26 Mar 1921, page 4.
12) Fiore, page 147, Vol. 1.
13) Rosen, page 116.
14) *The Tennessean* (newspaper), Nashville, TN, 4 Sept., 1889, page one.
15) Fiore, page 12, Vol. 2.
16) Title of Article: John Devoti, one of Gen. Buckner's Scouts — saw Gen. Morgan Shot. *The Chattanooga*, TN, 9 May 1922- page 14.
17) Fiore, page 41, vol. 2.
18) *Richmond Times-Dispatch* (newspaper) Richmond VA, 27 Feb 1930-page 3.
19) Fiore, page 100, Vol. 2.
20) *The Tennessean*, Nashville TN, 23 Feb 1928, page 8.
21) Fiore, page 109,Vol. 2.
22) *The Tennessean* (newspaper) 8 Aug. 1902, page 7.
23) Fiore, page 119, Vol. 2.
24) *Chattanooga Daily Times* (newspaper), Chattanooga, TN, 19 Apr. 1905, - page 3.
25) Fiore, Page 166, Vol. 2.

Chapter Four
Couriers

In an age where there were no iPhones, Starlinks etc, messages were carried by couriers on foot or by horseback. The couriers played a vital role in bringing messages to generals, or political leaders, or heads of spy networks.

Mrs. Claude C. Chin's (wife)
While reading Mr. Chinn's obituary, I unexpectedly found out something about his wife: "During the war Mr. Chinn was shot three times and one bullet lodged in his leg above the knee, where it remained swollen, gangrene developed. He married a Miss Petit during the war. Miss Petit was loyal to the Southern cause and carried dispatches between Confederate regiments." [1,2]

Andrew J. Frazier
"Andrew J Frazier, Confederate veteran, who often told that as a courier he carried General Robert E. Lee's order for Pickett's charge at Gettysburg, died at his home here today. He was 96 years old." [3,4]

Frank M. Ironmonger
"He entered the Confederate army at the age of 12 and served as courier boy during the last fourteen months of the War Between the States. One of his prized possessions was a medal declaring him the youngest enlisted soldier in the Confederate army." [5,6] (He was a general in the United Confederate Veterans)

Major John Conway Moncure
"On April 8, 1864, at the Battle of Mansfield, the greatest battle ever fought on the soil of this state (Louisiana), Major Moncure carried messages across the storm-swept field between the headquarters of General Polignac and his superior officer, General Taylor, concerning the conduct of the pending battle." [7,8]
Not only was Moncure a courier for General Polignac (who was a real French Prince), he was also his chief of staff.

Annie Perdue Sebring

"Mrs. Annie Perdue Sebring, wife of Gen. W. R. Sebring. Is dead of paralysis. She served the Confederate cause very cleverly as a messenger in the vicinity of Memphis during the War Between the States. [9, 10]

Simon Mayer

Jewish courier who: "Simon returned from the war a hero. He had narrowly escaped being killed at the Battle of Franklin when a bullet passed through his hat but missed his head as he carried a message to Gen. Jacob H. Sharp when he served as acting adjutant…." [11]

Ada Benjamin Fairfax

Mrs. Fairfax was a lady who volunteered to be a courier: "When the young Asbury Harpending was returning from visiting President Jefferson Davis in Richmond, on board the same ship was Ada Benjamin Fairfax of Virginia. Asbury told Ada he was afraid of getting arrested at the San Francisco docks. She told him "men are so silly," she asked him to give her the letters, (incriminating letters from Jefferson Davis to California Confederate leaders). Which she took to her cabin and sewed them to her skirt. The police did indeed search Asbury and his luggage, while this brave Virginian Lady walked by him smiling. She not only saved Asbury's life, but also the lives of many Californian Confederate leaders too." [12]

Lillie Hitchcock

"As a young teenager, Lillie and her mother were traveling on the *Orizaba* (ship), along with Brent, Gwinn and Benham (California Confederates). These men had maps of US military installations, which could get these men hung for treason. Lillie hid these documents in her dirty laundry, just before US General Sumner had them illegally arrested. Sumner was also aboard that ship." [13]

Betsy Duvall

"General Beauregard desperately needed to know when General Irwin McDowell planned to attack. Among the couriers Rose (Greenhow) used to send messages was the beautiful Betsy Duvall. Duvall crossed into Confederate lines with a tiny packet hidden in her long hair. In the packet was a note. When deciphered, said: McDowell has certainly been ordered to advance on the sixteenth. R. O. G. (Rose O'Neil Greenhow). General Beauregard had his reinforcements on time from General Joseph E. Johnston, and the South won the battle (First Manassas)." [14]

William Murrell (black messenger)

"Murrell is a Southerner, born and bred. No man who followed the tune of *Dixie* was ever more intense a Southerner than William Murrell, colored native of Georgia … and ex-Confederate veteran. His occupation of today was his occupation of forty-two years ago. A messenger now for a federal cabinet officer, he was in 1861, at Montgomery Alabama, a messenger for the first Confederate cabinet. He was engaged as such by Judah P. Benjamin, attorney general of the Confederate States." [15, 16]

Emmett P. Marable

"Emmett P. Marable 86, a Confederate veteran who served as a courier during the War Between the States, died Tuesday at a Lynchburg Hospital." [17, 18]

Antone W. Radescich

"He served as a courier for General Robert E. Lee during the War Between the States." [19, 20]

Notes

1) Title: C. C. Chin, Confederate Veteran, dies of wound-union bullet at last proves fatal. *The Indianapolis Star* (newspaper), Indianapolis, Indiana, 13 Sep. 1911 - page one.
2) Fiore, page 31, Vol. 1.
3) *The Salt Lake Tribune* (newspaper), Salt Lake City, Utah, 30 Apr. 1936.
4) Fiore, page 57, Vol. 1.
5) Title: Confederate aide of General Lee dies. *Long Beach Press Telegram* (newspaper) Long Beach, CA, 8 Dec 1939.
6) Fiore, page 84, Vol. 1.
7) *The Times* (newspaper) Shreveport, LA, 23 Jan., 1919, page 1.
8) Fiore, page. 115, Vol. 1.
9) *Tampa Bay Times* (newspaper) St. Petersburg, Florida, 13 Nov. 1913- page 1.
10) Fiore, page 146, Vol. 1.
11) Book: *The Jewish Confederates*, Robert. N. Rosen, University of South Carolina Press, 2000, page 341.
12) Boyias, page 10.
13) Boyias, page 6.
14) Davis, 1985, page 26.
15) *The Chattanooga News* (newspaper), Chattanooga, TN, 27 July 1903, Page 1.
16) Fiore, page 119, Vol. 1.
17) *The Roanoke Times* (newspaper) Roanoke, VA, 14 Nov. 1930- page 4.
18) Fiore, page 106, Vol. 2.
19) Title of Obituary: Courier for Lee dies at Winfield. *The American Progress* (newspaper), Hammond LA, 27 May 1937- page 1.
20) Fiore, page 139, Vol. 2.

Chapter Five
Staff

Introduction

When the scouts returned from their search to find the enemy's army, usually they brought the information that they discovered to the attention of their general's staff officers. It was the duty of these staff officers to evaluate the reports and forward these to the commanding general. In some cases really good scouts reported to the general directly. Staff role was to make sure that the commanding general knew at all times where the enemies army was.

The following are once again the names of staff officers nobody has ever heard of.

James W. Carter

"Colonel James W. Carter, native of Virginia and a member of the staff of General Robert E. Lee during the latter part of the civil war died … today at the age of 82 years." [1,2]

Colonel William Winston Fontaine

"Colonel William Winston Fontaine attached to the staffs of General "Stonewall" Jackson and General J. E. B. Stuart during the War Between the States, died at his home here today, aged 84." [3,4]

Major Thomas B. Gatch

"Major Thomas B. Gatch, probably the last surviving Confederate Marylander who served on the staff of General Robert E. Lee and Lieut. General Thomas J. Jackson died today at his home. … He was 94 years of age." [5,6]

General R. S. Hoke

"General R. S. Hoke, Ranking Confederate officer and personal choice of General Lee to succeed him in case he was killed in battle died on this morning at his home at Lincolnton, NC." [7,8]

General George P. Moormam

"He was on the staff of Forrest and others commanders during the war. Earning many special mentions and was commander of Moorman's Cavalry battalion." [9,10]

Major Jean Sosthene Mouton (Cajun)

"He was a member of that band frequently called the "Lafayette Prairie Boys," with whom he remained until he was appointed major on the staff of General Alfred Mouton. He was present at the Battle of Mansfield, when his kinsman General Mouton was killed." [11, 12]

Roland A. Painter

"Roland A, Painter 94 years old, Confederate veteran who served for seven months during the civil war as General Robert E. Lee's private secretary, died last night." [13, 14]

J. B, Ratcliff

"J. B. Ratcliff, 95, last known surviving member of General Taylor's staff in the Confederate army." [15, 16]

Dr. James Power Smith

"Funeral services for Dr. James Power Smith last member of the staff of Stonewall Jackson." [17, 18]

Major Jacob F. Stonestreet

"Major Jacob F. Stonestreet who served with the Confederacy during the war on the staff of General Jo Shelby." [19, 20]

Count Edward Von Lorisch

"During the civil war the Count served the Confederacy under the name Heineke as an aide to General Beauregard and captain of a company of the second Louisiana Rifles." [21, 22]

Major W. E. Wailes

"William E. Wailes Chief of Staff of General Joseph Wheeler in the Confederate Army during the civil war, died at his home in Dalton Georgia, yesterday." [23, 24]

Lieutenant William B. Meyers (Jewish)

"Will Meyers served as a lieutenant, as an engineer, and as an adjutant for Major Generals Samuel Jones and William W. Loring …Deleon has him as an adjutant to General John C. Breckinridge." [25]

Lieutenant Octavius Cohen

This Jewish officer did the following; "Cohen served in the signal corps in Savannah. In June 1862 Cohen fought at Secessionville while serving as a volunteer aide to Gen. William Duncan Smith, second in command to Brig. Gen. Nathan "Shanks" Evan's." [26]

R. L. Crawford

"He enlisted in the Confederate forces in 1861 and served throughout the war. He was on the staff of General Ledbetter during Bragg's Kentucky campaign and in the last years of the war was signal officer on the staff of General Daniel W. Adams." [27, 28]

W. G. Grove

"Grove a native of Virginia, was an aide to Robert E. Lee during the civil war. He came to California in 1867 by boat, the trip requiring more than 20 days." [29, 30]

McHenry Howard

"McHenry Howard, a grandson of Gen. John Eager Howard and Francis Scott Key (he wrote our national Anthem), Confederate veteran, lawyer and real estate man, died yesterday. Mr. Howard served through the civil war as an ordinance officer and later as a staff officer under Gen. George Steuart." [31, 32]

Major John Wyatt Jones

"Major John Wyatt Jones, one of the last Confederate staff officers, is dead in St. Louis, MO. His commission as major is said to have been the first issued by Jefferson Davis as president of the Confederacy." [33]

Robert Edmund Lee, Jr.

"The third son, now about twenty-six years of age (his father is Robert Edmund Lee, Robert E. Lee's half-brother). Served during the war on the staff of Jeff Davis, and subsequently on that of his cousin, General Fitzhugh Lee." [34, 35]

Ezekiel Norman

"He was attached to the staff of Stonewall Jackson, and was on guard duty at Chancellorsville the night the Southern leader was accidentally shot by his own men." [36, 37]

Captain John Taylor Wood

"Captain John Taylor Wood, who was a grandson of President Zachary Taylor, and a nephew of Jefferson Davis, died here today, aged 74 years. During the civil war he was with the Confederate army, and served as colonel on the staff of Jefferson Davis." [38, 39]

C. W. Custis Lee

His father was Robert Edmund Lee, Robert E. Lee's half-brother: "C. W. Custis Lee served as aide-de-camp to Jefferson Davis for some time during the recent war." [40, 41]

S. H. Mitchell

"He was reared in the state of Georgia and when only 16 years of age he enlisted in the Confederate Army and was assigned to the service of General "Stonewall" Jackson. For quite a while during the war he was an orderly to General Jackson." [43, 44]

Captain Augustus Pifer

"After Virginia seceded he returned to his native state to enter service of the Confederacy. He was appointed commander of General Robert E. Lee's staff and captain of his bodyguard, known as Lee's Scouts, guards and couriers. In which capacity he served until the surrender at Appomattox. He received wounds at Gettysburg." [45, 46]

Robert A. Webb

"Robert A. Webb, 83, a member of General Lee's staff in the Confederate Army, died at his home, Saltillo, Mississippi." [47, 48]

Colonel William Harrison Werth

"Mr. Werth's father, the late Col. William Harrison Werth, was a member of President Davis' staff at Richmond and later commanded the 49th Virginia Infantry in the War Between the States." [49]

William A. Asburn

"According to the book *Surry County Soldiers in the Civil War*, my 3rd great grandfather William A. Asburn was a courier for General Jubal Early while with the 53rd NC Infantry." [50]

Notes

1) *Pine Bluff Daily Graphic* (newspaper), Pine Bluff, AR, 24 June 1921- page 4.
2) Fiore, page 29, Vol. 1.
3) *Arkansas Gazette* (newspaper), Little Rock, Arkansas, 3 Nov. 1917- page 16.
4) Fiore, page 56, Vol. 1.
5) *The Los Angeles Times* (newspaper) Los Angeles, CA, 26 Dec 1933- page 1.
6) Fiore, page 60, Vol. 1.
7) *Wichita Daily Times* (newspaper), Wichita Falls, Texas, 5 July 1912, page 4.
8) Fiore, page 78, Vol. 1.
9) *The Irvine Leader* (newspaper), Irvine, Kansas, 19 Dec 1902, page 1.
10) Fiore, page 117, Vol. 1.
11) *The St. Helena Echo* (newspaper) Greensburg, Louisiana, 30 Oct. 1896 - page 3.
12) Fiore, page 118, Vol. 1.
13) Title: Gen. Lee's private secretary dies, Oakland, CA, 25 May 1936, page 3.
14) Fiore, page 125, Vol. 1.
15) Title: Another Confederate Dies, *Corsicana Daily Sun* (newspaper), Corsicana, Texas, 22 Nov., 1930- page 7.
16) Fiore, page 137 Vol. 1.
17) T*he Brownsville Herald* (newspaper), Brownsville, TX, 7 Aug 1923- page 1.
18) Fiore, page 151, Vol. 1.
19) *Moberly Monitor-Index* (newspaper), 21 June 1932, page 2.
20) Fiore, page 157, Vol. 1.
21) *The Baltimore Sun*, Baltimore, Maryland, 6 April 1901, page 8.
22) Fiore, page 171, Vol. 1.
23) *Houston Chronicle* (newspaper) Columbia, SC, 6 June 1915, page 2.
24) Fiore, page 172, Vol. 1.
25) Rosen, page 92.
26) Rosen, page 94
27) *New York Tribune* (newspaper, 12 Sept. 1921- page 9.
28) Fiore, page 34, Vol. 2.

29) *The Fresno Bee* (newspaper) Fresno, CA, 8 Feb 1943-page 9.
30) Fiore, page 65, Vol. 2.
31) *The Bee* (newspaper) Danville, VA, 12 Set. 1923, page 3.
32) Fiore, page 80, Vol. 2.
33) *Boston Evening Transcript* (newspaper) Boston, MA, 31 July 1903- page 14.
34) *The Philadelphia Inquirer*, Philadelphia, PA, 13 Oct. 1870, page 4.
35) Fiore, page 99, Vol. 2.
36) *The News Journal* (newspaper) Wilmington, DE, 6 Dec. 1932- page 11.
37) Fiore, page 123, Vol. 2.
38) *The Baltimore Sun*, (newspaper), Baltimore, MD, 20 July 1904- page 8.
39) Fiore, page 1 82, Vol. 1.
40) *The Philadelphia Inquirer* (newspaper), Philadelphia, PA, 13 Oct 1870, page 4.
41) Fiore, page 99, Vol. 2.
42) *The Covington Leader* (newspaper) Covington, TN, 18 at 1922, page 2.
43) Fiore, page 118, Vol. 2.
44) *The Atlanta Journal* (newspaper), Atlanta, GA, 20 May 1907 -page 2
45) Fiore, page 133, Vol. 2.
46) *Cleveland Plain Dealer* (newspaper), Cleveland, OH, 15 Feb, 1927, - page 22.
47) Fiore, page 180, Vol. 2.
48) *Evening Star* (newspaper) Washington, 10 April 1943-page 6.
49) Fiore, page 181, Vol. 2.
50) Book: *Surry County Soldiers in the Civil War.* (North Carolina) By J. D. Lewis, 2004-2005.

Chapter Six
Partisan Rangers

Introduction

Partisan rangers did collect information on where the enemies armies were, just like the scouts. The scouts did occasionally use their pistols, shotgun and carbines. However, the partisan rangers routinely were aggressive, routinely carried out attacks on supply trains, sabotage on railroads, camps, and installations. They were indeed spies, and special forces all wrapped up in one dangerous package. Here are many of these unknown and forgotten partisan rangers heroes.

Andrew Jackson Bobo
"Word was received of the death of Andrew Jackson Bobo aged nearly 89 years at his home near Kessel, WVA. Mr. Bobo was a member of the McNeil Rangers, the Confederate band that made a raid on Cumberland toward the close of the war and took the union Generals Crook and Kelley prisoners, capturing them, in their rooms in the hotels, at that time 10,000 Federals were encamped at Cumberland." [1, 2]

Joseph W. Davis
"Mr. Davis was born in Bowling Green …. and served in the Confederacy during the entire war. … He joined John Morgan's command and served during several campaigns with him." [3, 4]

Captain Peter Everett
"Lexington, KY — Capt. Peter Everett, a noted Confederate, aged sixty five and an associate of General John Morgan in the civil war, died here today in an asylum." [5, 6]

Thomas H. Grimes
"Thomas H. Grimes 88, Confederate Veteran who served under Morgan's command." [7, 8]

Colonel John S. Ewart
"Home burnings during the war were very frequent in the county, and one of those was that of a strong Confederate partisan. He was Col.

John S. Ewart whose home near the Beckley water company dam was burned by union men during the war." [9]

Captain L. D. Hockersmith

"Captain L. D. Hockersmith who is reputed to have dug his way out the Columbus, Ohio, penitentiary during the civil war and to have liberated his commander the General, John H. Morgan, with a number of his men, died at his home here, aged 82." [10, 11]

Frank James (Jessie's brother)

"They became the two most daring raiders of the band, their hearts were filled with hate of the Northern cause and its soldiers and friends and they slew and reeked in blood. They lived only to kill and avenge. They learned how to ride a horse at full speed, the bridle in their teeth (reins), a revolver in each hand, which was the way of the guerrillas. They learned how to shoot from the back of a galloping horse and never miss the mark. Their lives were spent in the brush hiding, or riding on long raids at night to be early in the morning at the passage of some band of federals. They hunted and were hunted. They knew no fear. They had great adventures and narrow escapes. They laughed at death and rode into the very face of it, screaming the Quantrell yell, which froze the blood of those that heard it." [12, 13]

Colonel Roger Moore

"In the spring of 1862 he entered the service again as a member of the company known as Lawrence's partisan rangers." [14, 15]

Solomon Mullins

"He also served under General Morgan in some raids through the southern highlands." [16, 17]

John W. Overton

"He was a member of Col. John H. Morgan's command during the civil war and was a valiant soldier." [18, 19]

Harry W. Piper
"Harry W. Piper, Confederate veteran and one of general John Hunt Morgan's men died at his residence." [20, 21]

Colonel James T. Ripy
"Colonel James T. Ripy 78, retired and distiller and Confederate veteran during the civil war, died today of pneumonia. He served under the command of General John Hunt Morgan, famous raider." [22, 23]

H. C. Rogers
"General Rogers was born in Kentucky and was prominent in the service throughout the conflict between North and South. He was a member of Morgan's Cavalry." [26, 27]

Captain Robert C. Scott
"Scott served as a captain in the Confederate Army under General. Morgan, during the entire war. He was a brave soldier." [28, 29]

Major M. A. Spurt
"He enlisted in the Confederate service in September 1862, becoming a member of Troop A, Eighth Kentucky Cavalry. He was with his outfit on Gen. John Morgan's celebrated raid in 1862, and was captured with his commander and most of his men at Buffington Island. He was placed in prison at Camp Chase, Columbus, Ohio, with many others of Morgan's men but effected his escape along with about 100 others." [30, 31]

John Sutton
"He joined the Confederate army in the early part of the civil war and served under General Morgan, Mr. Sutton took part in the invasion of Indiana, which caused so much excitement in that part of the state in those days, but was captured and imprisoned at Columbus, Ohio, where he later escaped." [32, 33]

Colonel Edwin Warren Moise
Jewish Colonel who raised and commanded his own Cavalry company, *The Moise Raiders*. One of the best known of the family's Confederates (related by marriage) was a daring and intrepid Cavalry officer Colonel Edwin Warren Moise of Charleston.

In May 1862, he raised his own cavalry company of partisan rangers." Mainly at his own expense, at the cost of his entire holdings ($10,000). The 120 man company is called *The Moise Rangers* one of several military companies named after Jewish Confederates, and it became Company A, 7th Regiment of Colonel William Claiborne's Confederate Cavalry. … In February 1864, the Moise Rangers attacked and captured a union gunboat the *Smith Briggs*, turning its gun on nearby Federal boats and driving them away.

Moise also served with the legendary and renowned Cavalry Corps commander Major General Wade Hampton, with whom he became close friends, on various operations,including the famous "Great Beef Steak Raid" in which they captured 304 prisoners and a huge cache of supplies, including some 2,500 head of cattle. By early 1865, Moise's unit was attached to the 10th Georgia Cavalry battling Sherman's Army as it marched into South Carolina during the last desperate days. He led the attack on Major General Judson Kilpatrick's (his nickname was kill Cavalry), forces at the "Battle of Kilpatricks Pants." Because the General was caught unawares and forced to flee his camp in his bedclothes." [34]

Moise's company was not the only company named after a Jewish officer. Joseph Benjamin, the brother of Judah P. Benjamin (acting Secretary of State), had a cavalry company named after him.

Another officer Samuel Yates Levy's also is rumored to have had a company named after him." [35]

Spenser Roan Thorpe

"During the civil war he served the Confederacy, being captain of a Kentucky regiment under the command of General Morgan." [36, 37]

Dr. G. W. Walker

"Dr. G. W. Walker was only 14 when he entered the service in 1862 and he served three years. He was in Gen. Morgan's command." [38, 39]

Sergeant Jas. H. Bozarth
Captain W. J. Taylor
Private Walter Morgan's -Partisan -Rangers

Rarely do we find descriptions of a skirmish, but in this case we were lucky: "Among the incidents that illustrate in a striking way the steady gallantry of individuals, one in which the participants were Capt. W. J. Taylor, Sergt. Jas H. Bozarth and private Walter McDaniell, all of company A, deserves to be recorded. "In the spring of 1865, all of the Kentucky regiments, infantry and cavalry had become so depleted by casualties in battle, by disease, that the authorities gave them the only opportunity to recruit which was open to them. They went back to Kentucky but at this late time in the war, they found no recruits and so returning they found that they were being followed. To add to their discouragement, the murderous and bloodthirsty Burbide was in command in Kentucky, and his orders to shoot as spies all Confederate soldiers caught here was in force. A cavalry troop was known to be in dangerous proximity behind them. The alternative of surrendering or running this perilous gauntlet was before them.

They chose the latter, then spurred their jaded horses and dashed forward as bullets whistled them from right, left and rear. They formed the desperate resolution to make a stand and give battle, turning abruptly through a passable way into one of the fields … and faced about as Taylor exclaimed: "We will fight them here." They sat with drawn revolvers to await the coming of their pursuers into close range. Six well mounted men dashed in open order upon them. They were armed with carbines and pistols and led by an officer of whose gallant bearings his three foes spoke admiringly, there was no confusion, no sign of retreat on either side, but the grim silence was suddenly broken by a clash of carbines and revolvers. When it ceased there were six empty saddles. Five federal cavalrymen lay dead or dying, and the officer, whose horse had been shot under him, stood dismounted and mortally wounded. The pursuers were either too much excited by the chase or they lacked the skill, for the three Kentuckians were untouched." [40, 41]

Charles N. Burr

"Mrs Lorena Burr, 75 of Herndon, was married to Charles N. Burr. She was 16 years old when they wed and he was a widower many years her senior. Mr. Burr lived in Herdon all his life except during the civil war when he fought for the Confederacy. About all she remembers of her husband's role in the war is that he belonged to Mosby's raiders, as did many Fairfax county youth." [42, 43]

Anderson D. Chamblin

"He enlisted in the Confederate Army when 16, and served for 18 months as a member of the Spartan Rangers." [44, 45]

Frank Chinn

"Frank Chinn, 79 years old, a member of Morgan's Cavalry in the civil war." [46, 47]

Dr. John A. Wyeth (16 years old)

"Dr. John A. Wyeth, author of the *Life of Forrest*, was with Morgan's Cavalry for some months at liberty, having his own weapons, but not allowed to join." (only 16 years old). [48, 49]

Charles Jacob Cameron (1838-1876)

"My three (times) great grandfather, started the war as a first lieutenant in the First Virginia Cavalry. After an ankle sprain and many months of furlough and light duty, he was not reelected as an officer, he enlisted as a private in the 62 Virginia Mounted Infantry Regiment serving with "Imboden's Rangers" for part of 1862." [50]

George W. Crystal

"George W. Crystal 89 years old. a member of Morgan's Cavalry and a native of Fayette County. He was captured in 1862 by Union troops in Ohio during one of Morgan's raids, and was held prisoner until his release May 5, 1865." [51, 52]

Captain M. J. Kirk

"Partisan Rangers — those who desire a good opportunity to join the partisan service are referred to the notice in this morning's issue, of captain M. J. Kirk, commanding Partisan Rangers, Pocotaligo, SC." [53, 54]

Jared A. Harral

"Mr. Harral was a native of Russellville Ala., but moved to Texas, while very young. He recruited a company for General T. N. Waul's Texas Legion in the war, but because of his youth, 19 years, he yielded his position as captain to B. J. Hogue. Later he served with General Forrest's Cavalry and was commended for his heroism at Fort Pillow and Pittsburg, Miss." [55, 56]

Frederick Southgate Hipkins

"He served throughout the war under General Mosby." [57, 58]

Thomas Bell Poole

"Trooper Poole was a member of Captain Rufus Henry Ingram's guerrilla band (Northern California). They were betrayed when one of his troopers couldn't shut up. Eventually, they were ambushed by a sheriffs posse at Almaden Road. Poole was shot in the face and was arrested at a place called Somerset House. Poole was tried, convicted, and hanged at the Placerville jail, five months after Lee surrendered at Appomattox. [59]

Captain Rufus Henry Ingram

During the War Between the States there were many robberies of gold shipments in California, some of these robberies were committed by Confederate guerrillas. The only reason we know about Captain Ingram's guerrilla band is because one trooper had a big mouth and as a consequence the band was ambushed by a sheriff's posse. The band was shot to pieces, Captain Ingram escaped with the gold, some died, some were captured and one trooper Thomas Bell Poole (a former lawman), was shot in the face and was eventually hanged in a Placerville jail. We will never know how many of these robberies were in fact committed by Confederate guerrillas. Nor will we ever know how many of these gold shipments ended up in Richmond. [60]

Frank Green — Andrew King

Both were leaders of the "Monte Boys," a heavily armed secessionist militia group of more than 70 horsemen. El Monte is an area south of Los Angeles, where most of the men were also members of the secret organization "Knights of the Golden Circle." The ultimate goal was to establish a cattle empire in Northern Mexico. The city of El Monte was peopled at that time by transplanted Texans. And was a hotbed of Southern secessionists and a dangerous place to those loyal to the Union. [61]

John B. Prout

"Mr Prout during the civil war was a member of Mosby's Rangers, having enlisted at the age of sixteen years. He was taken a prisoner at Upperville VA, November, 1863, having been betrayed, along with ten comrades, by a former ranger, who had been court-martialed, but who escaped to the Union lines." [62, 63]

John Underwood
"He is distinguished, above all other men whom I have known, by a wonderful faculty which enabled him to thread with unerring certainty, in the darkest night, the intricate forests and tangled brushwood of the country in which he lives." [64]

Lieutenant Fountain Beattie
"Fountain Beattie, Mosby's best friend and most trusted Lieutenant." [65]

Sergeant James F. "Big Yankee" Ames
"The Rangers thought they were simply going on another of their midnight forays, ambushing enemy troops and frustrating Union forces. Mosby had not communicated the nature of the mission to any of the men except the recent arrival of sergeant James F. "Big Yankee" Ames, who only weeks earlier had been a member of the Union army. Mosby would place his entire trust in this deserter and rely on him to get his men through Union checkpoints. They were attempting to pass through a gap in the pickets into enemy territory guarded so heavily that no one "dreamed of the possibility of an enemy approaching them," with the intention of capturing Colonel Percy Wyndham." Wyndham was a British soldier of fortune, who had called Mosby, "a horse thief." Wyndham, was not there, but General Edwin H. Stougton was! He was captured instead. [66]

Major William Hibbs
"One of Mosby 's earliest rangers was a local volunteer, "major " William Hibbs, a disheveled, gray-haired, middle-aged blacksmith with small black eyes." [67]

Ranger Dick Moran
"Shortly after dawn … A piercing voice shouted, "mount your horses! The Yankees are coming."' By running into Miskel farm, where Mosby's men were sleeping, by screaming Moran saved the whole troop from being captured or destroyed." [68]

Trooper Harry Hatcher
During this very same fight at Miskel Farm: "Harry Hatcher, nicknamed "deadly," … Handed Mosby the bridle (reins) of his horse, the

partisan leader mounted it and rushed into the melee, Hatcher soon vaulted onto a captured horse and joined the fight." [69]

William Chapman

In this same skirmish: "Some of the Yankees charged with sabers, but most employed their Remington pistols which in some cases misfired. In one such instance involving ranger William H. Chapman who, with his brother, Sam, rode with Mosby, both antagonists "weapons were a foot apart when they discharged" The Yankee's snapped, but Chapman's did the deadly work. He fired six shots and emptied five saddles." [70]

Sam Chapman

(William's Brother) In this very same skirmish: "Sam Chapman, a former divinity student, swung into action, after emptying both barrels of his pistols, he drew his saber and rode to the front of the Confederate ranks, "standing straight up in his stirrups, dealing saber slashes to the right and left. ..." [71]

Captain Bradford Smith Hoskins (British Soldier of fortune)

Same engagement: "Wearing the scarlet uniform of a British officer Captain Bradford Smith Hoskins joined Chapman and also slashed and hacked the federals with his saber. Hoskins had joined Mosby's command as a volunteer in March. A soldier of fortune (mercenary) ... unlike Mosby, he wasn't a teetotaler, spending St. Patrick's day downing "whiskey, punch, and sentiment." He missed the train in the morning in consequence." [72]

Private Richard Paul Montjoy

This incident occurred during the Grapewood Farm Engagement, when Mosby's little cannon was about to shoot at a disabled train; "As Chapman was about to pull the lanyard and fire the gun; private Richard Paul Montjoy, a swarthy and handsome Mississippian, previously with the famed (notorious) Louisiana Tigers before joining Mosby's command, screamed, "goodness! You will all be scalded to death. Move back seventy-five yards. Terrified of the deadly steaming water from the engine, the rangers wisely fell back." [73]

Willie Mosby (young brother) — French Dulany

He (Mosby) was then joined by his eighteen-year-old brother, Willie, within a week, he conducted another daring raid into the heart of federal-occupied Northern Virginia, in Alexandria. Mosby hoped to bag the provisional Governor of Virginia Francis H. Pierpoint. But the governor traveled to Washington that night, to Mosby 's dismay. So instead Mosby and his men rode down Telegraph Road to Rose Hill plantation. Colonel Daniel F. Dulany made the mistake of opening the front door. Mosby asked in a polite tone; "Is this Colonel Dulany? "Assuming the Confederates were Jessie Scouts, (Blazer Union scouts often wore Confederate uniforms.) Announced, "My name is Mosby." While the stunned Dulany stood silent, absorbing the gravity of the event, he recognized his son, French Dulany, a member of Mosby's Rangers. The war had pitted thousands of families against each other. Upon seeing his father, French exclaimed, How do pa I 'm very glad to see you. Well, Sir, I'm d____d sorry to see you." [74]

Captain Billy Smith continues "Captain Albert M. Hunter, an officer in Cole's Cavalry (Union), raided the heart of Mosby's Confederacy Rector Town. ... Captain Billy Smith collected nearly three dozen rangers and went after the Union troopers. ... Smith ambushed Hunter at Five Points. ... Forming a line of battle, the Union troopers occupied a strong position and fired their carbines at the oncoming horsemen, but many of the cartridges were damp from the inclement weather and misfired. Smith rode in front of his troops and ordered his men to charge to gain "the bulge." Screaming as they charged into the Union flanks and rear, the rangers unleashed a torrent of lead from their colts. Smith's second charge broke Hunter's men. Hunter later remembered his premonition the night before, "dreaming a dream that was realized the next day. The rangers routed the federals, killing, wounding, and capturing." [75]

General John Echols
Head of Intelligence

"In addition to raids on supply trains, the irregular unit (Thurmond's Rangers) acted as cavalry in the Confederate Army as the war progressed, often serving under General John Echols, and later were designated the 44th Virginia Cavalry Battalion. Six-foot-four Echols towered over most of his men in both stature and education. A Virginia Military Institute-Harvard educated lawyer and member of the House of Delegates on how the military is before offering his military service to his home state of Virginia. Echols had extensive battle experience before his assignment in Appalachia. The Virginian deployed the rangers in various activities such as scouting, conducting reconnaissance, and warning the Confederates of Federal attacks in the area.

The rules of war do not apply to Thurmond's rangers because they were guerrillas and no mercy was shown them, lamented one officer in the 23rd Ohio. The scouts (Jessie Scouts) were formed for just that purpose." [76]

Lewis Thornton Powell

On an autumn day in October 1863, a tall well-built, dashing young private with striking blue eyes … a nineteen year old Floridian, had been wounded at Gettysburg and admitted to a Union field hospital with a gun shot wound in his right wrist and a broken arm. Using his charm … he managed to wrangle a position as an orderly. His outward appearance belied an inner "ferocity of character." It is suspected that after befriending and likely seducing a sympathetic secessionist nurse, Powell acquired a Yankee uniform and escaped … the nurse was Margaret "Maggie" Branson. Branson's father was an operative for the Confederate Secret Service. Their boarding house doubled as a safe house for the clandestine service, the shadowy organization which specialized in spy craft, election interference,  communications, sabotage, and other forms of unconventional warfare. Very little is known about Powell's involvement with the group at this time, but within days, the masquerading Union soldier made his way to Scuffleburg and Mosby. Powell had a flair for escape and kept his cool during dicey situations. Once when the house he was boarding in as one of Mosby's Rangers was surrounded by Union Cavalry, Powell " blacked" his face with lampblack and walked out of the house. A complex soul, Powell also had a softer side. He was generous and liked children and animals. But his ruthlessness and effectiveness allegedly earned Powell the moniker "Lewis the terrible." [77]

John D. Walker

"He rode with the famous Confederate General John Hunt Morgan of Lexington on daring raids in Kentucky. ..." [78, 79]

Charley Binns

"Charley Binns, a Ranger deserter, had guided Reed's patrol (Union) that day. Binns a native of Loudoun County, fled Mosby's command after the guerrilla leader had him arrested for attempting to kidnap two free black women and sell them into slavery ... after Binn's escape and betrayal, Mosby's men could not wait to get their hands on him, so he skedadled during the action: "when the first shot was fired, Charley started to run and was never heard of by the Californians or our men. It was said that he stopped for one night in Winnipeg to get a bite and then went on towards the North Pole" [80, 81]

Captain John Breckinridge Castelman

Captain Castelman was a close friend of Captain Hines and was his second in command of the vast so called the Northwest Conspiracy insurrection. [82]

Colonel George St. Leger Grenfel

The Colonel was a British soldier of fortune and a veteran of four wars, who introduced discipline in the ranks. [83]

Acting Master John Yates Beall, CSN

Beall was a Confederate naval hero, who boarded and took over the only federal gunboat that was patrolling Lake Erie. His attempt failed he was convicted of piracy, but he avoided the hangman's noose by being exchanged for the return of federal officers held by the Confederacy. [84]

James Shanks

This agent betrayed Captain Hines, and became a traitor when he went to the commandant Colonel Sweet of Camp Douglas. Hines planned to free the Confederate prisoners languishing there. [85]

Lieutenant John W. Headley

One of the Confederate agents who tried to kidnap Vice President Andrew Johnson. [86]

Colonel Robert M. Martin

The colonel commanded the raiders who tried to burn down New York City in 1864. [87]

Ted Boyias

Aaron Burton
Mosby's trusted black servant, friend, courier and partisan ranger. [88]

Notes

1) Bobo Andrew Jackson: *The Capital Times* (newspaper), Madison, Wisconsin, 3 Feb 1929 - page 1.
2) Janet Fiore, page 14, Vol. 1.
3) *The Courier-Journal*, Louisville, KY, 10 Feb 1907, page 4.
4) Fiore, page 41, Vol. 1.
5) *The Indianapolis*, Indiana, 21 Nov. 1900, page 2
6) Fiore, page 51, Vol 1.
7) *The Lexington Herald*, Lexington, Kentucky, 29 Aug. 1932, page one.
8) Fiore, page 67, Vol. 1.
9) Title: Citizens prisoners were seized in this county by union troops. *Beckley Post-Herald* (newspaper), Buckley, WV, 26 Aug. 1950.
10) *Washita Valley Gazette* (newspaper), Chickasaw, OK, 7 May 1915- page 8.
11) Fiore, page 77, Vol. 1.
12) Title: Frank James, Began as a Wartime …. *Centralia Fireside Guard* (newspaper), Centralia, Missouri, 26 Feb. 1915, page one.
13) Fiore, page 85, Vol. 1.
14) Title: Death of Col. Roger Moore, *The Wilmington Morning Star*, (newspaper), Wilmington, NC, 22 April 1900, page one.
15) Fiore, page 116, Vol. 1.
16) Title: Last of Dickenson Confederates, *The Post*, (newspaper), Big Stone Gap, VA, 22 July 1937- page 6.
17) Fiore, page 119, Vol. 1.
18) *Nashville Banner*, Nashville, TN, 9 Apr. 1915, page two.
19) Fiore, page 124, Vol. 1.
20) Title: Service Held for Morgan Veteran, *The Cincinnati*, Ohio, 19 Nov. 1928 - Page 2.
21) Fiore, page 129, Vol. 1.
22) *The Billings Gazette* (newspaper). Billings, MT, 12 Feb.1922, page 7.
23) Fiore, page 139, Vol. 1.
24) Title: Virginia Landowner was a member of Mosby's Cavalry During the Civil War. *The Baltimore Sun* (newspaper), Baltimore MD, 26 Dec 1929 - page 13.
25) Fiore, page 141, Vol. 1.
26) *Lexington Leader* (newspaper) Lexington, KY, 20 Sept. 1930, page 8.
27) Fiore, page 141, Vol. 1.
28) *Lexington Weekly Intelligence*, Lexington, MO, 15 Feb. 1879.

29) Fiore, page 146, Vol. 1.
30) *The Nashville Banner* (newspaper) Nashville, Tennessee, 18 July, 1922, page 10.
31) Fiore, page 154, Vol. 1.
32) T*he Owensboro Messenger*, (newspaper), Owensboro, KY, 5 Mar 1920, page 4.
33) Fiore, page 159, Vol. 1.
34) Unpublished manuscript, by Lewis Regenstein.
35) Rosen, page 116.
36) *Los Angeles Herald* (newspaper), Los Angeles, CA, 5 Sept 1905, page 16.
37) Fiore, page 164, Vol. 1.
38) *The McAlester News-Capital* (newspaper), 25 May, 1936, page 8.
39) Fiore, page 172, Vol. 1.
40) Title: A War Story- Interesting account of Confederates who fought for their lives in open field. *The Twice A Week Messenger*, Owensboro, Kentucky, 18 June 1898- page 3.
41) Fiore, page 16, Vol. 2.
42) *The Evening Star* (newspaper), Washington, DC, 25 Apr. 1955- page 23.
43) Fiore, page 21, Vol. 2.
44) *The Virginian-Pilot* (newspaper), Norfolk, VA, 1 July 1923-page 21.
45) Fiore, page 27, Vol. 2.
46) *The Owensboro Messenger* (newspaper), Owensboro, Kentucky, 23 May 1922-page 3.
47) Fiore, page 28, Vol. 2.
48) *Nashville Banner* (newspaper) Nashville, Tennessee, 2 Nov 1914- page 12.
49) Fiore, page 30, Vol. 2.
50) Unpublished Manuscript by Liam Opie.
51) *The Courier-Journal* (newspaper) Louisville, Kentucky, 28 October 1934-page 14.
52) Fiore, pace 35, Vol. 2.
53) Ad or notice in: *The Daily Confederate* (newspaper), Raleigh, NC, 10 Feb 1864- page 2.
54) Fiore, page 57, Vol. 2.
55) *The Atlanta Journal*, (newspaper), Atlanta, Georgia, 31 Dec 1933- page 10.
56) Fiore, page 70, Vol. 2.

57) *Times Union* (newspaper) Brooklyn, NY, 17 Dec 1923- page 2.
58) Fiore, page 76, Vol. 2.
59) Boyias, page 5.
60) Boyias, 2023, page 34.
61) *The Star* (oldest newspaper in Los Angeles), 2 February, 1861.
62) *The Evening Star* (newspaper), Washington, DC, 8 January 1913- page 4.
63) Fiore, 137, Vol. 2.
64) O' Donnell, page 21.
65) O' Donnell, page 25.
66) O' Donnell, page 26.
67) O' Donnell, page 35.
68) O' Donnell, page 37.
69) O' Donnell, page 38.
70) O' Donnell, page 39.
71) O' Donnell, page 39.
72) O' Donnell, page 42.
73) O' Donnell, page 43.
74) O' Donnell, page 53.
75) O' Donnell, pages 62-63.
76) O' Donnell, page 66.
77) O' Donnell, pages 66-67.
78) O' Donnell, page 86.
79) *The Buffalo News*, (newspaper), Buffalo, NY, 21 July 1893.
80) Fiore, page 177, Vol. 2.
81) O' Donnell, page 119.
82) Munson, *Reminiscences of a Mosby Guerrilla*, page 90
83) Horan, page 84.
84) Horan, page 4.
85) Horan, page 151.
86) Horan, page 151.
87) Horan page 151.
88) O'Donnell, page 354.

Conclusion

Unlike the federal secret service that at first was run by the Pinkerton's and other centralized federal departments in Washington, the Confederate Secret Service was only nominally under the leadership of President Jefferson Davis. In name only, but in fact it was a series of independently run intelligence networks, both civilian and military throughout the whole South. There were some active in Richmond, but these networks were every where the invading Union Armies were, following the invader's every move. The scouts were mostly Cavalry scouts, who constantly reported to their commanding generals or to their general's staffs. There were thousands of civilian volunteer scouts who also provided a constant stream of information to the Army scouts about the enemie's location. There were scouts on foot also, and the civilian scouts were predominantly folks who you would never suspect as being spies. General Forrest had a young farm boy riding his mule go through enemy lines gathering valuable information. We have heard of many instances of young pretty girls gathering intelligence (Wild Rose Network) or acting as couriers, like Betty Duvall and Belle Boyd.

This constant flow of accurate information as to the various union armies whereabouts, allowed brilliant generals such as Stonewall Jackson, Nathan Bedford Forrest and many others, to strike at will at the yankees who regularly outnumbered the Confederates three to one or even four to one. Good generalship combined with surprise attacks and patriotic fervor when you are fighting to defend your land, your people and your kinfolk, brought forth the series of victories.

President Davis had his private intelligence network which reported directly to him, just like the networks run by Secretary of War and State Judah P. Benjamin. For the most part there was no centralized Confederate Secret Service. And in fact, the Confederacy survived as long as it did, because of this constant flow of accurate intelligence, from this decentralized system of independent civilian and military intelligence networks all over the South.

These people, civilian and military scouts, risked their lives to gather this valuable information about the whereabouts of different union armies. And quite a few in fact made the ultimate sacrifice by getting hanged like Sam Davis, or shot by the Federals. Unfortunately, many others were hanged, tortured or executed in prisons like the Old Capitol Prison in Washington, DC, and other federal prisons and jails throughout the country.

The purpose of this book is to find the names of these heroic Southern patriots. For those who were lucky to make it through the war alive, and for those who were not so lucky, and who made the ultimate sacrifice. It is extremely hard to find out about these unknown hidden heroes as they shunned publicity and hid in the shadows. It should be made known this was a very brutal war going on secretly between Confederate and Union spies. There was not much mercy shown. People were killed on both sides, which created an atmosphere of violence, retaliation, similar to feuds which went on during the war. Surprisingly, these revenge killings continued after Appomattox up until at least 1868 and further. We must find more of these heroes. Make their names and their sacrifices known throughout the country, and properly honor our great heroes.

God bless the heroes of the Confederate Secret Service and God Save the South.

Bibliography

1) Boyias Ted: Book: *California Knights of the Golden Circle/ Their Dream of a Pacific Republic-* Revised Edition. The Scuppernong Press, 2023.

2) Davis, William C.: Book: *Spies, Scouts, and Raiders- Irregular Operations During the Civil War.* Alexandria, Virginia, 1985, page 24.

3) Ellsworth, George A: Book: *Everything is fair in war: The civil war memoir of George A. "Lightning" Ellsworth, John Hunt Morgan's Operator.* Register of the Kentucky Society 108, nos 1, 2, pages 3.

4) Fiore, Janet Lindeman: *Self Professed Confederate Obituaries and U.S. Newspaper Mentions.* Volume 1, first printing 2024

5) Ibid, Volume 2

6) Horan James D.: *Confederate Agent- A Discovery in History*, The Fairfax Press, MC M LIV

7) Lewis, J. P.: Book: *Surry County Soldiers, North Carolina, 2004-2005.*

8) Mills, Harold W: Book: *The Confederate Secret Service, 1861-1865.* Covenant Books Inc, Murrells Inlet, SC, 2018.

9) Moses, Raphael, J: *Last order of the lost cause:The Civil War Memoirs of a Jewish family from the Old South*, University Press of America, 1995.

10) O' Donnell, Patrick K: Book: *The Unvanquished*, Atlantic Monthly Press, New York, 2024

11) Rosen, Robert N: Book: *The Jewish Confederates*, University of South Carolina Press, 2000

12) Talbott, Laurence F.: Book: *California In the War for Southern Independence*, The Scuppernong Press, Wake Forrest, NC, 2024.

13) Miller Francis Trevelyan: Book: *Soldier Life and the Secret Service*, Castle Books, New York, 1957

www.ingramcontent.com/pod-product-compliance
Lightning Source LLC
Chambersburg PA
CBHW050042080526
44586CB00014B/1421